The Fall of The Ethical Bank

Paul Gosling

© 2018 Co-operative Press Ltd

All rights reserved. No part of this publication may be reproduced, stored in a retrieval system or transmitted in any form or by any means, electronic, mechanical, photocopying, recording or otherwise without the prior permission of the publisher or in accordance with the provisions of the Copyright, Designs and Patents Act 1988 or under the terms of any licence permitting limited copying issued by the Copyright Licensing Agency.

Published by:
Co-operative Press Ltd
Holyoake House, Hanover Street
Manchester, M60 0AS, UK

ISBN-10: 197570083X

ISBN-13: 978-1975700836

Contents

Foreword 7
Chapter 1: Managing Decline 11
Chapter 2: Peter Marks 17
Chapter 3: Britannia 23
Chapter 4: Financial Misreporting 37
Chapter 5: Verde 45
Chapter 6: Moody's Killer Blow 61
Chapter 7: Demutualisation 71
Chapter 8: The Directors 79
Chapter 9: The End Game 87
Chapter 10: The End of the Road? 91
Index 103

Foreword

Ethics and the Co-op

The Co-operative Bank marketed itself as 'the ethical bank'. Yet – as with much else of importance that happened to the Bank, and its former owner, The Co-operative Group – this owed as much to accident as design.

The co-operative movement originated as a truly ethical initiative. The Rochdale Pioneers started the retail movement in 1844 to allow low-income families to buy nourishing, unadulterated food at affordable prices. That is about as ethical as a business can get.

Along the way, though, ethics and customer service often got sidelined in business. Parts of the co-operative empire forgot where it came from – and why it was there.

The Co-op Bank was no exception. My memory of the its Leicester branch in the 1980s was one of incompetence and customer anger. Lunchtime queues of people waiting to be served sometimes trailed out the front door onto the street. On occasion customers vented their anger. I remember one well-known labour movement activist, Alex Acheson, shouting out at staff from his place in the middle of the queue, 'for God's sake put more people on the counter at lunchtime, not less'. It seemed as if the customers knew more about how to run the business than the Bank's own managers did.

Simon Williams became marketing manager of the Co-op Bank in 1998, coming from a rigorous commercial background at senior levels of successful large businesses. He must have realised that – at the time – the Bank was well-known for having a poor public reputation. Its customer service was bad, some of its branches looked shabby and banking with it was more a self-imposed duty than a pleasure.

In those circumstances it was sensible that Williams asked its customers what they valued about the Bank. An alternative way of asking the question might have been, 'why on earth would you want to bank with us?'. The answers shocked the Bank. Overwhelmingly customers responded that it was the Bank's ethical policy. The trouble was, the Bank did not have an ethical policy.

Rather, what the Co-op Bank had was a customer perception that it had an ethical policy. Many customers (including myself) had moved to the Bank in the 1970s as the only UK clearing bank without a relationship with South Africa. People who wanted to boycott apartheid South Africa transferred to the Co-op Bank and stayed there.

As a response to this surprising market research finding, the Bank decided to turn perception into policy and rebrand itself as 'the ethical bank'. Alongside this, the Bank modernised branches, improved customer service, added a capital 'T' to The Co-operative Bank moniker and formulated a clear ethical statement. The headline was that the Bank would not accept customers who did dodgy business, such as arms dealers.

But promoting a business as being 'ethical' can be a hostage to fortune. Can a bank continue to market itself as ethical when it has been found to have mis-sold substantial numbers of personal protection insurance policies? Could it continue to do so after failing in its attempt to enter the notoriously ethically challenging market of independent financial advice?

Even more to the point, what happens when 'the ethical bank' is found to have been chaired by an individual who by day was a Methodist preacher, but at night time was found to have consorted with rent boys and taken crystal meth – becoming known in the tabloids as the 'Crystal Methodist'?

Yet it was not the issue of ethics that brought the bank down. In the wake of the financial crash and the publicity of what RBS, Lloyds and Barclays had been responsible for, those customers who valued ethics had few other avenues to go down. Even as late as 2017, the Financial Times reported that 85% of the Bank's customers cited the ethical policy as the main reason for their custom.

Ultimately, what did for the Co-op Bank was incompetence on a massive scale. Ethics – and the lack of it – comes into the story. But essentially this is a story of how bad managers destroyed a bank and how bad directors allowed them to do it.

CHAPTER 1

Managing Decline

When trying to understand the collapse of The Co-operative Bank, the place to start is The Co-operative Group. After all, the Bank itself was not actually a proper co-operative.

Rather, The Co-op Bank was a plc, wholly owned by The Co-op Group. A deep-seated malaise within the Group spread out into the Bank and caused it to crash. To understand this crisis at the Group it is necessary to understand some of its history.

When they opened their first grocery store in 1844, the Rochdale Pioneers found their local co-operative society was so successful that lots of other local societies sprang up to replicate it. Independent local societies were so effective that the co-operatives – taken together – became the UK's largest grocery provider up until the 1960s. But that is when things began to go wrong.

This successful legacy has been a burden for those that followed. No one wants to merely manage decline and attempts at recreating past glory have been an important factor in the later catastrophe.

In the 1960s, the grocery sector began to modernise – it became big and brash. National brands led by Tesco and Sainsbury's took market share away from the small local co-op societies. Where those big brands had economies of scale, local societies relied on their national buying organisation, the Co-operative Wholesale Society (CWS), to compete. It struggled to do that.

Within those local societies, it was hard to dislodge a mindset that was formulated in the good old days. Many store managers were resistant to change. Where Tesco and Sainsbury's rewarded innovation and invested in management training, many local societies did neither.

And the democracy that should have been an asset to the co-operative societies became a weakness. In principle, societies are owned and controlled by their members, the customers. This was the basis on which the dividend – the famous 'divi' – was paid. The more a customer spent, the bigger the divi payout.

But there was a cancer at the heart of that democracy. Staff could also be members. And senior managers not only encouraged staff to be members, but also often told them how to vote. In the annual board elections, this meant it was possible that the staff could be relied upon to outvote the customers.

As far as those senior managers were concerned, the last thing they wanted were independently minded directors, who would innovate, experiment and shake up the co-operative establishment. A very conservative breed of management demanded and obtained a very conservative breed of directors. And in retailing, being conservative is the road to decline.

CWS – *the graveyard*

Small local societies began dying out. Gradually, where there had been hundreds of societies – the total number estimated at 1,439 in 1900, often in the form of one society for a single town or village – these merged down to just a few regional societies. So, to prevent the co-op retail sector dying out, the CWS expanded its role. It had been set up as the buying, wholesaling and distributing arm of the local societies and of the national Co-operative Retail Services.

But gradually the CWS became more than just the wholesaler. It evolved into becoming a retailer, taking over struggling local societies. So as local societies gave up, their assets were transferred to CWS. The CWS became a graveyard for struggling co-operative societies.

To be a repository of failed businesses is a difficult place from which to operate. Add to that the often poor quality of local, regional and even national management, and it is easy to understand the nature of the CWS problem. Even worse, arguably, it was sitting on valuable historic assets from which it could live extravagantly for many years, wastefully using up a legacy built by generations of co-operators and failing to deal with deepening trading problems.

Inevitably, most co-op societies merged to strengthen their economies of scale. Even those that were doing well chose to amalgamate with other local societies. Over the years, regional societies grew alongside CWS, so that the UK retail co-op movement became a patchwork of regional societies that, for the most part, have managed to respectfully avoid competing with each other.

Merger was seen as the route to survival for the retail societies; bigger and bigger mergers took place. The biggest of all was in 2007 between the aggressive and ambitious United Co-operatives, which operated across Yorkshire, the North West and North Midlands, and the Co-operative Group.

And United's brash and very self-confident chief executive became – through his own negotiation – the new CEO of the combined organisation. Peter Marks was to imprint himself firmly on the future of the co-operative movement, including the Co-op Bank.

CHAPTER 2

Peter Marks

Peter Marks believed in himself. His vision was clear to everyone who knew him; he would shake up the stuffy co-operative movement and bring it into the modern business world.

One of his favourite sayings was: "The co-operative movement has two problems. It doesn't co-operate. And it doesn't move."

Others had equally pithy comments to make about Marks. One leading co-operative figure told me: "The thing about Peter Marks is that he wouldn't recognise a co-operative principle if it hit him on the end of his nose."

Marks was clear about his role. It was to bring the co-operative societies together – preferably as a single retail co-operative under his leadership.

It hardly needs saying that he was on bad terms with some other leading co-operative society chief executives. Within the Co-op Group, Marks was dominant. Few people argued with him. Even fewer stayed at senior levels within the organisation after they had argued with him.

Marks was driven by his belief in his role in co-operative history – he would go down as the person who would save the co-operative movement and drive it forward to new successes – and he would do so by achieving the economies of scale that had enabled competitor businesses to succeed. It was mergers that would rebuild the business.

The Somerfield deal

Peter Marks was a deal maker. He loved doing deals, and a deal with Somerfield seemed magnificent to him. To Marks' thinking, what the Co-op Group needed in order to compete was the ability to buy in quantities similar to those bought by the major brands, bringing down wholesale purchase prices and spreading logistical overheads across a broader operating base.

Through combining Somerfield with the existing Co-op Group turnover, he was taking the business "back into the big league", as he put it.

There was, though, a major fallacy with this idea. Over the decades, the Group had moved away from department stores to focus on grocery retailing.

And within this sector, the Group had abandoned the big hypermarket and supermarket operation that pitted it directly against Tesco, Sainsbury's, Asda and Morrisons. Instead, it had established a strong presence in the convenience store market – small shops serving a clearly defined local community. But Somerfield was located in a different market sector.

Somerfield stores were typically medium-sized, rather than small convenience shops – and at the time the mid-store sector was in the worst decline of all. It was neither the small local shop that serviced its neighbourhood or urban office workers, nor was it the big shop that offered big discounts and large car parks. It was neither one thing, nor the other.

Quite simply, the Co-op Group was buying many stores it could not use; and although it nearly doubled its market share, this would dissipate as many of those stores closed. Somerfield was bought in 2009 for £1.57bn, with capital raised through heavy borrowing that gave the bank lenders an unhealthy say in the way the Group was to be run in the future.

Paul Myners, who conducted an independent review of the Group's corporate governance in 2014, observed that there was "nothing to show for that deal". In short, it was a waste of £1.57bn, which cost even more because of the interest on the debt used to pay for the purchase.

Some of the acquired assets were in reality just very expensive liabilities. Many of the stores were on leaseholds with years still left to run, yet were too large to be retained as part of the Co-op Group's retailing strategy. The Group acquired 977 Somerfield stores, of which 600 were then vacated and on which lease payments were still to be paid – at an annual cost of £500m. This deserves a place in the pantheon of historically bad business deals.

The disastrous takeover undermined the viability of the Group itself. At this point the organisation consisted of various trading entities: banking, life assurance, commercial insurance, pharmacy, farming, funerals, legal services, travel, car sale and cash security, as well as food retail. It was in part because of the error in buying Somerfield – an apparently quick fix to an ingrained problem – that the Group, from 2013 to 2014, set about disposing of pharmacy, farms, and the Sunwin cash security business.

As the Group tried to raise cash, it also sold the life assurance operation in 2013 and attempted to sell the general insurance arm (there were no buyers at the price asked).

The Group's travel business had been merged with Thomas Cook in 2010, while Marks was in charge, and the Group subsequently sold its stake in this business, too, in 2016.

With the benefit of hindsight, it is possible to view the Somerfield acquisition as one of the worst ventures in co-operative history. Even so, it was not as destructively terrible as The Co-op Bank's takeover of the Britannia Building Society. And that was a deal with strong similarities to the Somerfield acquisition.

CHAPTER 3

Britannia

The Co-op Bank's decision to take over Britannia was not actually the worst UK banking deal of all time. That distinction clearly belongs to the Royal Bank of Scotland's purchase of most of ABN Amro in 2007 – just as the world's markets collapsed.

Lloyds' purchase of Halifax, soon afterwards, also destroyed more value than the Co-op-Britannia deal. For all that, the Co-op Group made a spectacularly awful decision in taking over Britannia.

Nor can it be said that this was a short-term fix that went wrong: the Group made a conscious decision and it had planned for it. It was a very bad call.

The evidence that there had been long-term thinking behind the deal comes from the passing of the so-called Butterfill Act (properly called the Building Societies (Funding) and Mutual Societies (Transfers) Act 2007). This piece of legislation allowed, for the first time, different types of mutuals to merge. The proposer of the Bill was Sir John Butterfill. When interviewed by the author he declined to say who was behind the legislation, simply indicating that his constituency contained business operations owned by large mutuals, which needed greater flexibility.

This was true – he represented Bournemouth, which was home to a very large call centre run by the Liverpool Victoria Friendly Society. However, Liverpool Victoria denied to the author that it had any involvement or interest in the Act.

Sir John told me (for an article in Co-operative News) that the link-up between Co-operative Financial Services (CFS) and Britannia is "absolutely the type of thing we are looking at". He added: "I don't think you will find them alone."

But behind the scenes, one well-placed source said, it was the Co-op Group that had pushed to ensure the Bill was drafted and then enacted. And the Group (through its Co-operative Financial Services subsidiary, which owned the Co-op Bank) was one of only two institutions to use the Act.

In fact, it might be said that the Act has been a disaster for the co-operative and mutual movement. While the intentions were good, the applications have been bad.

It certainly seemed to make sense for friendly societies and building societies to merge, for example – except that there is no sign that there is any interest in those two sectors in coming together.

The lesser-known application of the Butterfill Act involved the Kent Reliance Building Society, a struggling organisation that over-loaned in the boom times and then was at risk when the downturn came.

While other damaged building societies sought rescues within the sector, Kent Reliance used the Butterfill Act in a very different way.

The private equity business JC Flowers had sought entry into the UK's banking market. In order to do this, it established a supposedly mutual subsidiary, which then effectively took over Kent Reliance. This combined business now operates as OneSavings Bank and is a FTSE 250 plc. The Butterfill Act had demutualised a building society – not at all what lawmakers had been told it would be used for.

The second application of the Butterfill Act was the Co-op Bank's takeover of the Britannia Building Society. As with the Somerfield deal, the driving force was Peter Marks. This committed deal-maker adopted one overarching principle into his business philosophy: "Achieve scale." He believed the Co-op should stay in sectors where it could grow to achieve competitive scale and exit business lines where scale was not possible.

In the mind of Peter Marks, The Co-operative Bank had to achieve scale. The Bank had become the Group's cash cow – its profits were central to the profitability of its parent organisation. But the Group – under Peter Marks' leadership – got greedy. The assumption was probably that the financial sector would just keep growing. It was an error of judgement of similar scale to that of Gordon Brown when he boasted that his economic policies had brought to an end the economic cycles of boom and bust. The truth is that economic cycles persist – and when the cycle goes down, the financial services sector suffers.

But during those good days of persistent economic growth, various building societies were eyed up for acquisition by the Group and Bank.

For a while, the Norwich and Peterborough Building Society looked like the most attractive takeover target. But a closer look at the figures worried both the Group and the

Bank. (Norwich and Peterborough was eventually rescued by Yorkshire Building Society in 2011.) Britannia seemed the most attractive proposition.

IT investment

Before the Britannia deal entered the pipeline, CFS was already gearing up for the future. In the Co-op Bank's 2007 financial report, it recorded an investment of £250m – five times its operating profit for the year – in new systems, to ready itself for expansion. Part of this was for Project Finacle, an IT system which, the Bank claimed to me at the time, would create the most advanced technological base for any bank operating in the UK at the time. These preparations for expansion were led at Group level by Peter Marks and at CFS and the Bank by its then chief executive David Anderson and then chair Graham Bennett.

(Graham Bennett was a co-op movement insider – he was chief executive of the Southern Co-operative and had been a Bank board member since 1989. His predecessor was Alan Prescott, who was chair from 1996 until 2000, when Bennett took over. Prescott was a senior executive at CWS, prior to it becoming The Co-operative Group, while being chair of its subsidiary. The heavily criticised Paul Flowers became chair of the Co-op Bank in 2010, just after the Britannia merger.)

The IT system was intended to do much more than just service the Bank. For a start it was for CFS – which was seeking to be an integrated bank, insurer and life assurer. The IT system was intended to be the technological base for fully integrating those businesses and also to bring the Bank and insurer much closer to the Group. The view of the Group was that very lucrative cross-selling opportunities could be achieved through a more integrated technological base.

Unfortunately there were two barriers to realising that dream. Firstly, the so-called 'bancassurer' model had failed where other banks had tried to implement it. Much of the financial services sector had thought that banking and insurance could and should be brought together as natural partner products. Yet customers were not persuaded. Over the coming years, various insurance businesses acquired by banks were sold as owners gave up on the idea. The Co-op believed it would succeed where others had failed.

Secondly, regulators were uncomfortable about close connections between a food or general retailer and a bank. Regulators wanted some degree of separation. Just as the Group was seeking closer links between the business lines through an integrated IT system, regulators were looking for a Chinese wall between them. Rumours suggested the Labour government was seeking to exercise influence over the regulators to prevent a stronger separation being imposed on the Co-op Group from CFS.

The IT investment immediately preceding the takeover of Britannia suggests a confused trading strategy. It may also hint that the board of the Bank were led by the Bank's (and Group's) executives in developing strategy – the wrong way round.

If so, however, both the executives and board were guilty of having no clear and consistent business strategy. A further, and even more worrying, indication of where the power lay comes from the fact that negotiations between the Bank and Britannia were well advanced and reported in the press before they were reported to the board. Lord Myners was dismissive of the quality of both the Group's and the Bank's boards. Senior executives also had a low opinion of both boards at the time and seemed to believe they should take the key decisions themselves.

There was another problem with the IT investment. It was predicated on CFS integrating the banking and insurance businesses closer together, rather than expanding the Bank's mortgage-lending business. Meanwhile executives were considering exactly the opposite strategic direction – expanding mortgage lending through merger with a building society (ie a mortgage lender).

The merger with Britannia meant the IT investment had gone in the wrong direction and needed to be fundamentally reshaped to cope with a much-expanded loan book; the new system was ill-equipped for the growth of business which the Co-op Bank now needed. This raised serious doubts about the £250m IT investment in 2007.

But expanding the sale of CFS insurance products had been one of the main arguments for the deal on the CFS side. Britannia sold Legal & General (L&G) and Axa insurance products, while CFS 'manufactured' its own insurance products. With the Britannia brand selling CFS products in place of L&G and Axa, CFS would have strengthened its sales significantly.

When I interviewed Britannia's then-chief executive Neville Richardson at the time, he told me there was a clear rationale from Britannia's point of view behind the merger. "We need better internet capability," he said.

"CFS has that through Smile. We need better transactional capability and the Bank has its current account. We outsource loans and credit cards. CFS does those. There's a lot in it for Britannia."

However, Britannia saw the relative strengths of the two institutions in different terms from how CFS saw it. While CFS believed it was the dominant body, Britannia saw itself as an 'equal partner', stressing that each organisation had about three million members.

That difference of perception was the basis for continuing cultural conflict within the merged Bank. Even at the stage of merger negotiations, potential future tensions were being revealed.

Richardson chose to regard CFS as a relatively independent body within the Co-op Group's structure, rather than as a subsidiary that could be instructed by the Group.

Richardson explained at the time: "CFS operates within the co-operative movement, but with appropriate levels of autonomy, as are required by the Financial Services Authority ... The view we have taken is that we would only look at it if it was a merger of equals."

Where the Britannia deal went wrong

Hindsight provides a wisdom that is often unavailable at the time. And that is the widespread view about the Britannia deal. "If only people had known the dangers," it is said. That general view is also that due diligence was not done which would have enabled CFS to understand the liabilities that Britannia brought with it – as if the failure of due diligence was some uncontrollable act of God.

(Due diligence, it should be explained, is a normal part of a merger or acquisition. Accountants and lawyers go in and check that the values on the balance sheet are correct, that the liabilities shown are not understated and that the assets are accurately valued. That process will check, for example, whether large amounts of debts owed to the business are at risk of never being repaid.)

However, this view of the Britannia deal is less hindsight and more the rewriting of history. It is worth examining some contemporaneous reporting.

My own 2008 report (for my Co-operative News column) explained: "There has been speculation that Britannia could have difficulties with above-average lending for a building society in buy-to-let mortgages through its Britannia Capital Investment Group subsidiary. But this interpretation is dismissed by Britannia, which points out that its bad debt and write-off levels in the recent period have been below those of CFS. It says that its buy-to-let business has avoided high risk investments and focused on loans that are sustainable, whatever happens in the property market."

The Financial Services Authority (FSA, the regulator at the time), had already privately warned Britannia that it was concerned about the high-risk nature of its operations – a much higher risk profile than the Co-op Bank was willing to be exposed to prior to the deal.

In effect, the acquisition of Britannia would transform the risk profile of the Bank: from low risk before the deal, to high risk afterwards.

Sir Christopher Kelly's review of the financial crisis at the Bank, published in April 2014, reported: "The FSA raised issues relating to the long-term sustainability of Britannia's high-risk model in an ARROW letter in early 2009. It expressed concerns about Britannia's Illius business [which acquired for re-sale repossessed properties], which it deemed not core to the activities of a building society as well as being an imprudent use of funding and beyond the capabilities of the Britannia management. It subsequently transpired that the FSA had placed Britannia on a watchlist. Two years later, in July 2011, the regulator told the Bank that 'Britannia would have failed had it not been for the Co-op'. But at the time the FSA apparently did not consider the merger to be a rescue."

Nor, apparently did the FSA consider it necessary or appropriate to warn the Bank's board of what they were getting themselves into. Sir Christopher's review also found that Britannia's executives and board were unaware of the FSA putting the society on a 'watchlist' – regarding themselves as a well-managed and successful business.

Yet given the concerns that were in the public domain, it was more important than ever that effective due diligence took place on Britannia's loan book. Except, it didn't. For reasons that have never been adequately explained, due diligence was superficial.

Remarkably and unusually, it was CFS itself that undertook responsibility in-house for examining the most sensitive Britannia loan books. And that was only done at a high-level basis, without close examination of the actual loans, the current market value of the underlying assets and the history of repayment.

Britannia told the Bank it was determined to avoid awareness of the potential deal, thus requiring little pre-deal activity within its offices, as would be involved in proper and effective due diligence.

There was obvious excitement about the opportunity from the merger. "It's a terrific opportunity to create a new large mutual force," said the then CFS chief executive David Anderson. That excitement perhaps simply drowned out the caution.

But that is no excuse for the lack of due diligence. What is more, the CFS auditor, KPMG, had been instructed to undertake specific acts of due diligence – but not on the parts of the Britannia business that were to be found to be seriously weak.

This in-house due diligence was overseen by the finance director of CFS, Barry Tootell. No one properly investigated the scale of potential losses that the Bank would take over from bad lending decisions by Britannia - and about which there was already wide gossip.

The board was reassured about the scale of the due diligence. They were told by their deal advisors, J.P. Morgan Cazenove, that the level of due diligence was high and above that normally involved in a merger between listed public companies. Apparently J.P. Morgan Cazenove gave this opinion based on assurances provided to them by the Bank and by Britannia. It was enough to satisfy the Bank's board.

The Bank of England's Prudential Regulatory Authority (PRA) has since been clear where it placed the blame for this failure. "Mr Tootell did not oversee adequately the financial due diligence process on the Britannia Corporate Loan Book to ensure that it adequately identified and documented the risks inherent in the book and which may have impacted on the capital position of the firm," it said.

The most generous interpretation of the mood at CFS – and within the parent Co-op Group – is that ambition got in the way of sense. Executives, and subsequently non-executives, became blinded by the thought of the positives, so they were unable to see the nasty reality.

The ambitious vision was that this new bank would achieve the 'scale' that Peter Marks aspired to. The combined financial services organisation would have around £70bn of assets and 13,000 colleagues. While Britannia was the much bigger mortgage lender, CFS contributed most of the assets and staff.

Meanwhile, Britannia would also provide a much larger branch network. This was just at the time, it should be remembered, that the internet and mobile banking made branch networks more of a liability than an asset.

In the early years following the financial crash, CFS congratulated itself on avoiding the pain. Back in 2007 and 2008 it seemed as if the crash was all about capital instruments that no one – including the boards of the major banks – understood. These included mortgage-backed collaterised securities, with undeservedly high credit ratings. CFS had avoided these products and so thought it had avoided the big impact of the market crash, which at the time was termed the 'credit crunch'. "We have a very clear principle that any new instrument goes through a very strong process of approval," CFS's then chief executive David Anderson said at the time in an interview with the author.

With the benefit of hindsight it is possible to spot complacency here. The knock-on impacts of the crash in the value of complex securities led onto a big reduction in the value of real assets, such as properties that acted as collateral for lending by both CFS and, in particular, Britannia. It seems that the executives of the two financial institutions were oblivious to this.

In addition, the credit crunch reduced the availability of funds and so made borrowing more expensive – squeezing margins and profitability. The hit on profitability was made even worse as central banks cut base lending rates – it is much more difficult for banks to make profits in periods of low interest rates.

But the mistakes in the Bank/Britannia deal were on both sides. CFS walked into the deal with its eyes shut. Britannia's executives – led by the building society's CEO Neville Richardson – and non-executives might have been excused for having a party to celebrate. As far as the then regulator the FSA was concerned, Britannia was a failing institution that was being rescued by CFS.

There is an echo in the CFS takeover of Britannia from past events at the Group. Don't forget, back in 2007, the CEO of the smaller United Co-operatives, Peter Marks, had become CEO of the merged Co-operative Group.

So too in 2009, Neville Richardson the CEO of the smaller and financial troubled Britannia, managed to insert himself as CEO of the merged CFS. Anderson, a highly respected CEO of the profitable CFS, took retirement.

The view within CFS was that Richardson was appointed CEO as a condition of the merger. It was a considerable feat of negotiation by Richardson. Barry Tootell became finance director under Richardson and later went on to succeed him as interim chief executive.

The FSA reported that Tootell was not impressed by Richardson. "Richardson had not been the most suitable candidate for CEO of the merged CFS-Britannia entity, which he [Tootell] felt should have been David Anderson," noted the FSA. "[Tootell's] view was that it had been an acquisition not a merger but Richardson's position as CEO was a requirement of the deal proceeding."

And Andrew Bailey, the FSA's then director of regulation for banks and building societies, spelt out his opinions of Richardson and the merger in a meeting in July 2011.

Minutes record that Bailey "set out his view that Britannia would have failed had it not been for the Co-op and

Richardson had been lucky to survive, not least as CEO of the merged entity. He [Bailey] said that FSA continued to have issues with the effectiveness of the [Co-op Bank's] Group's Risk Management and controls and he was not persuaded that Richardson had ever grasped those issues. Consequently, [Bailey] was unconvinced that Richardson would ever fix them."

Despite this, the Group and the Bank's boards were apparently bullish about the merger. At this point the Bank had a new chair, Bob Burlton, a senior figure in the retail co-operative movement. He was chair, briefly from 2009 to 2010, while the Britannia acquisition went through.

"This move will accelerate the momentum within the co-operative and mutual sector," said Burlton. "Both businesses have been pursuing successful strategies independently and are strong in their own right but we recognise we could be even more successful by coming together to create the UK's most trusted financial services business."

CHAPTER 4

Financial Misreporting

The idea of a merger is to create a new institution stronger than those separate bodies were before they came together. This was not the case when the Co-op Bank took over Britannia – though that fact did not apparently occur to the Bank for a few years.

Even when this truth should have been apparent in the Bank's financial results, it was not.

By July 2011, the FSA had become extremely concerned about the capital strength of CFS as the body which technically owned the Bank. In an extraordinary meeting between the regulator and the Bank's full board and senior management team, the FSA's Andrew Bailey spelt out the scale of the crisis. The FSA reported that Bailey "wished to use the opportunity to provide the Board with strong messages about the Bank's capital position, the serious concerns that FSA retained following the significant misreporting of its liquidity position and on the weaknesses in CFS's risk management."

Just as shocking as the financial misreporting was the scale of the capital shortfall at the Bank. This was known by its board and by the regulator before this entered the public domain.

The FSA told the Bank – again in July 2011 – that, regarding its capital adequacy, "CFS's position was low relative to its peers. Although the Bank met its regulatory requirements, its level of capital meant its ability to withstand shocks was limited. Since it had limited access to capital, it was reliant on the broader Co-operative Group for support."

Bailey explained that "it had come to light that CFS had significantly overstated its liquidity position by misreporting the maturity of corporate accounts".

Neville Richardson responded angrily that he was "affronted" by FSA's accusation that there had been "wilful" misreporting.

In its later review of the financial crisis at CFS and the Bank, the PRA concluded that the Bank did not have adequate risk management systems. That failure, said the PRA, had reduced the Bank's resilience and its capacity to withstand difficulties.

According to the PRA, the Bank had breached a principle required by the regulators with regard to its risk management systems. "The Co-op Bank's control framework was inadequate... [It] did not have adequate risk management framework policies and procedures in relation to corporate lending and capital management; and the management information produced by the firm, including management information for its board, was not adequate. It was not sufficiently forward-looking and did not sufficiently highlight the key issues."

Much of the blame for these reporting failures has been placed on Barry Tootell as finance director. Tootell was regarded as the key person with responsibility for these functions. Tootell, said the PRA, breached his specific responsibility "which provides that an approved person performing an accountable function must exercise due skill, care and diligence in managing the business of the firm for which he is responsible in his accountable function".

In a key part of the PRA's commentary on Tootell's failings, it said: "Between 22 July 2009 and 10 May 2013, Mr Tootell was centrally involved in a culture which encouraged prioritising the short-term financial position of the firm at the cost of taking prudent and sustainable actions to secure the longer-term capital position of the firm. Mr Tootell was centrally involved in the firm managing its finances and capital position in a manner that was not in line with its stated cautious risk appetite and prudent bank management more generally."

There were a series of detailed failures in the financial management of the Bank, which strongly contributed to its crisis. In July 2009, when Tootell was the senior executive responsible, there was a change in accounting treatment of some financial instruments which "significantly boosted the firm's short-term capital position at the expense of its medium and longer-term position".

But the assumptions used for the financial reports proved to be incorrect, damaging the Bank's subsequent financial position and market reputation. Tootell was also the senior executive responsible for artificially boosting the Bank's capital position and for optimistic provisioning of the corporate loan book inherited from Britannia. Nor did Tootell "take adequate steps" to inform the Bank's board of directors of any of these matters, including its due diligence weakness and true capital position of the Bank. That due diligence failure was also pinned, to a large extent, on Tootell.

"Mr Tootell did not oversee adequately the financial due diligence process on the Britannia Corporate Loan Book to ensure that it adequately identified and documented the risks inherent in the book and which may have impacted on the capital position of the firm," said the PRA.

Moreover, when Tootell later became chief executive of the Bank he became aware that this loan book was a significant risk to the capital position of the Bank and that the Bank needed a new strategy to deal with this. Instead, though, he "did not exercise adequate oversight in order to ensure that a clear, comprehensive and effective strategy for the corporate loan book was adequately developed and implemented by the business".

Assessments of the fair value of Britannia's corporate loan book were inadequate, took too little time and involved reviewing too few loans. The valuations were not subsequently revised when there were opportunities to do so and reductions in the book value of the loan book were "at the lower end of potential adjustments", the PRA decided.

Tootell has been blamed as significantly responsible for failings that led to the near collapse of the Bank and, by implication, for part of the associated financial crisis at The Co-operative Group. But there was also a wider cultural failure of lack of challenge that operated in much of the Group and Bank. The PRA noted that "the Co-op Bank's culture resulted in an environment in which some staff felt under pressure to meet impairment forecasts that had previously been set". This is an important point to recognise, as it makes clear that short-term financial pressures are not unique to companies seeking to influence their stock market values – they can affect co-operatives as well.

Tootell was a professional accountant, a member of the Institute of Chartered Accountants in England and Wales (ICAEW). As such, he was subject to the regulation of the Financial Reporting Council (FRC). It meted out a withering judgment on Tootell in 2016, excluding him from membership of the ICAEW for six years.

Tootell failed, said the FRC, to "exercise due skill, care and diligence in managing the firm" and "was knowingly concerned in the contravention by the Co-op Bank of Principle 3 of the Principles of Business, in that it failed to take reasonable care to organise and control its affairs responsibly and effectively, with adequate risk management systems." The FRC also noted that the misconduct "was not dishonest, deliberate or reckless" and that "Mr Tootell was not solely responsible for the Misconduct". However, "the Misconduct was repeated and occurred over an extended period of time".

Also in 2016, the PRA published a final notice against Tootell, which provided more detail of the criticisms of his leadership of the Bank. Core failings were a culture that prioritised short-term financial positions and in which there was a lack of internal challenge. Significantly, the failures also included not reporting properly and adequately to the board.

In addition to the sanctions imposed by the FRC, the PRA prohibited Tootell from holding a significant position in any authorised firm. Tootell was fined £173,802 and also had to pay £20,000 costs towards the FRC investigation. Keith Alderson, the former managing director of the Co-op

Bank's Corporate and Business Banking Division, was also prohibited, while being fined £88,890.

For Tootell, this is presumably the humiliating end to his professional career.

Gareth Rees QC, executive counsel to the FRC, commented: "The period of exclusion imposed in this case sends a clear message to accountants of the high standards of professional conduct expected of them when undertaking important roles within business. The sanction reflects the significance of the misconduct by a CFO and CEO of a major UK bank, and the need to promote public and market confidence in the accountancy profession and the quality of corporate reporting in this sector."

It would be wrong to suggest that any single individual is solely responsible for the financial crisis at the Bank. The PRA found Keith Alderson to also have serious culpability. But the FRC is not investigating any other professional accountant with regard to the Bank's near collapse, though at the time of writing it is investigating KPMG's audits of the Bank.

A spokesman for KPMG responded that, given the public interest and other inquiries taking place into the Bank, it was no surprise this was being extended to the Bank's audits. He added: "As auditor to the Bank we believe that we have provided, and continue to provide, robust audits which provide rigorous challenge to the judgements and disclosures proposed by the Bank's management."

CHAPTER 5

Verde

Peter Marks' quest for the Holy Grail of business scale was far from over, even with the takeover of Britannia anything but bedded down. Marks had another even bigger prize in his eyes – a large portfolio of 632 Lloyds Bank branches which, with their customers, was to be auctioned off under the TSB brand name.

The sale was under the instruction of the European Union as a requirement of state aid rules, as a result of the government's rescue of Lloyds. The process was kick-started in 2011.

There were arguments for and against the potential deal, named Project Verde. At a stroke, the Co-op Bank would obtain an additional 4.8 million accounts, of which 3.1 million were personal customers, potentially giving the Co-op 7% of the UK personal current account market.

There was, though, no guarantee that the customers would stick with the Co-op after the transfer – many might quickly migrate back to Lloyds, or indeed move to another bank. Some might even be angry at the enforced transfer and jump as a protest.

Then there was the whole question of whether it was sensible to take on a commitment of a large branch network. The Co-op had to date expanded its customer base with the support of its award-winning internet brand Smile, which enabled the Bank to grow without a large branch network.

Meanwhile competitor banks were undertaking the difficult task of wholesale branch closures. Was it sensible for the Co-op to be swimming against the tide on this? It had already rejected the industry's common approach by betting on bancassurance, just when all the other banks were betting against it.

In addition, the Co-op Bank's IT system was a difficulty. Bringing together the Co-op and the TSB customers – who would stay on the Lloyds system for an interim period – presented technological problems. It would also mean the need to write off previous major investments in IT by the Co-op. Further, it would mean a dependency on another bank's IT hardware for some time.

Capital was another problem, but the complex Project Verde deal potentially came with its own capitalisation from Lloyds. So it was hoped that regulators would accept the capital adequacy rules were met.

For all these arguments for and against, it came back once more to a single idea – that businesses need scale. The Co-op should only be in business lines where it has scale, the thinking went – and it should exit those business lines where it does not have it. So the Co-op went for the big time in Project Verde and it felt a bit like an all or nothing gamble – success or fail. It seemed like all the chips were being placed on one square. Except almost everything had already been lost on the Britannia bet and apparently no one had yet noticed.

'We are not betting the Bank'

The board – or the majority of the board who were dominated by some Bank and Group executives – were convinced that the Verde deal was right for the Bank and did not constitute a high-risk venture.

I interviewed the man who took over as chair of The Co-operative Bank, Paul Flowers, just after he took office. He was what is termed 'larger than life'. He was a big man – overweight, to be blunt. He was extremely personable, very friendly, and came to his Co-op Bank role with a reputation. He was an influential figure in both the Co-operative Party and the Labour Party and, while chair of the Bank, was an adviser to the then Labour Party leader Ed Miliband on financial services and industrial policy.

Flowers had been a senior councillor in both Bradford and Rochdale and deputy chair of Rochdale council social services committee. The appointment of Flowers was not because of his banking background – though he had been a bank clerk in his much younger days – but because of his engagement in the co-operative movement and ethical commitment as a Methodist minister. The key factor in his favour was as someone with recognised skill for chairing committees and achieving group agreement in difficult circumstances. However, Flowers soon became damaged by rumours within the organisations. The phrases 'expense account', 'hotel rooms' and 'rent boys' were circulated. Group executives presumably heard the gossip, which might have undermined Flowers' capacity to stand up to them.

I met with Paul Flowers over a nice lunch in an expensive Manchester restaurant – paid for on his Co-op Bank expenses card – after the Bank had put in its bid for Verde. I interviewed him at his request as he was keen to persuade me that Verde was a potentially good deal, aware of my scepticism. "We are not betting everything," he insisted. "Far from it, in fact. It requires investment, but nothing like the scale of investment that has been speculated about in the financial press."

Flowers strongly argued the case for the Verde acquisition. "The overarching strategy is still to offer a compelling co-operative alternative," he explained.

"That means we have to punch above our weight and make certain we achieve better scale, because a bank which currently has 2% of the domestic market of the United Kingdom – albeit with a bunch of really lovely customers who value what we do, and who value the Bank's services, and, in particular, a bunch of institutional customers, local authorities and others, who know we are a good bank – still is insufficient scale.

"If we are really going to offer a 'co-operative alternative', we need to achieve much greater scale, which is why the prospect of making a bid for the Lloyds TSB carve-out is quite crucial. We have had to weigh up – and are still weighing up – the pros and cons of that possible deal.

"We have put in a firm bid for the process, which we agreed at the board two or three weeks ago [early in November 2011], and we are awaiting a decision of the Lloyds' board on that matter. Two days ago [on the 23 November], Lloyds announced that there were only two bidders left in the process, which is ourselves – which happens to be the only bank with any scale – and NBNK, which is effectively a private equity outfit, led by Lord Levene and a number of other peers from the House of Lords."

There was a deep irony here for the co-op movement, as Lord McFall had taken on a role as a director of the NBNK banking operation bidding against the Co-op. Lord McFall as John McFall was a Labour/Co-operative MP and chair of the Treasury select committee. "I am saddened and disappointed that a former Co-operative MP has not seen the light," said Flowers. "But notwithstanding that, we are clearly the only credible bidder. The Lloyds board has to decide by the end of December whether to do a deal with ourselves or NBNK or to do what is called an IPO."

An IPO is an 'Initial Public Offering' – in other words floating the 632 branches that were up for sale as a separate new company on the stock exchange.

Flowers continued: "We are serious about wanting to do a deal that could offer us considerably greater scale, bring with it 632 branches – including the entire former Scottish TSB estate and the entire former Cheltenham & Gloucester estate – which would enable us to have a much greater presence within the home market."

The risk that customers would revert back to Lloyds, or transfer to another bank, after the Verde portfolio was acquired was dismissed by Flowers. He said that "we are a really good relationship bank" and that the Co-op's high quality of customer services would lead to it retaining the vast majority of acquired customers.

Flowers admitted the Verde bid did expose the Bank to risks. "There are always risks. In terms of the financing, it carries some risk. You never get anywhere in developing that sort of business unless you take some risks. If you look at co-op models in different parts of the country or the world, co-ops that have never taken any risks are mainly dead and buried.

"But the co-ops that have taken risks in order to develop the model and develop the business are the ones who get the prize of sustaining and developing their business. So, of course you must take some risks, but you must quantify it and understand what it is. And that is what we are trying to do.

"If we don't acquire the Lloyds TSB branches, then our strategy is still to grow organically and to still seek investment of several hundred million pounds over the next few years, to enable the bank branch network to grow, to roughly 500 branches, as opposed to the roughly 340-odd [that it had at the time] and to clearly target certain areas of primarily current account customers – private individuals – and to clearly target institutional customers as well. That takes a lot longer, so my clear preference is to do the sort of deal which is currently available, not withstanding that that brings with it some obstacles and some risks."

Flowers insisted there was sense in the strategy of growing the branch network when other banks were running theirs down. "You have to weigh up the relativities of how your customers do their banking," asserted Flowers. "Our branches are well run. We know that lots of our customers want to use branches and value the customer relationship and we are trying to develop the range of other products that we sell through those branches, as well as through the other channels, internet and telephone."

It was the prospect of cross-selling other financial products – particularly mortgages, but also insurance – that was behind the Bank's renewed focus on branch banking, despite swimming against the tide of industry thinking. "Branch banking ain't dead yet," stressed Flowers.

Flowers also spoke positively of the IT investment that had already taken place, much of which would have to be written off if Project Verde went ahead – and much of which had to be written off anyway, without Verde. "£750m of investment over a period of time is being delivered through the world-leading companies who do these systems, Infosys, based in Bangalore, and their partner Steria, based in Delhi," said Flowers. "Some of that has already been rolled out to general acclaim and happiness, particularly to our corporate customers and the rest of it is being rolled out in the next two years and will be finished by the end of 2013."

Flowers added that IT upgrade implementation was being overseen by a board sub-committee and independent experts. "We are doing our best to keep executives on the straight and narrow," said Flowers. "We will have a state-of-the-art IT platform that will be the best of any bank in the UK or Europe. That will lead, if all goes well, to a much higher level of cross-selling of products to customers and make it much easier for staff to understand customers."

Flowers added – in what now seems a spirit of hubris – that while the Co-op Bank did not want to be the repository of failed building societies, it would be happy to take over more societies. In fact, it did make an approach to Northern Ireland's Progressive Building Society. "If there are building societies in the future that want to associate themselves with us in building a vibrant co-operative sector then we will be very happy to talk to them and work with them, whatever form that work takes," he said.

But Flowers demonstrated his understanding of the challenges facing mortgage lenders – and in doing so also demonstrated that the mainstream media caricature of him as someone completely out of his depth was wrong. "One has to question the future going forward for that whole [building society] sector unless they find a way of transforming themselves, not least when a number of them have been reduced in terms of their ratings to effectively junk bond status, which is where some of them are now at, which prohibits them from doing any sustained business in terms of capital markets and stymies their opportunity to do anything other than loans for mortgages and savings, the margins on which are tight. They have to examine where they are going."

Flowers emphasised the ethical basis of the Bank's operations. He explained: "We need to keep on reminding people that there are people who are providing financial services who do have a more ethical perspective. We are not perfect – who is? But we still need to try to provide something that people want to have, which is provided well and ethically."

Ironically, Flowers congratulated himself and his colleagues on having adopted a low-risk strategy.

"Actually, our model of doing business has not needed structural support," said Flowers. "We have been very liquid and very cautious and very prudent about how we run our business."

Then came the losses

For two years – 2011 and 2012 – Project Verde distracted the Bank and the Group. Meanwhile, rumours of the weak state of the Bank grew. The Bank's 2012 results – published in March 2013 – showed the game was up, but every insider played the game of pretence. For several years, the Bank's annual profits of £50m or so helped prop up the Group's figures. But for 2012, things went dark – very dark. The 2011 profit figures of £54.2m went deep into negative territory in 2012, with a reported loss of £673.3m. That loss consisted of an operating loss of £280.5m, which included impairments of £468.7m on the value of the Bank's assets, plus another impairment of £150m on intangible assets and provision of £149.7m for compensation for the mis-selling of PPI. The £150m recognised loss on intangible assets reflected that if the Verde deal went ahead, some of the past investments in IT were worthless – but if it did not go ahead, a new strategy would be required that also meant past investments were misguided.

In his annual chair's report, Flowers downplayed the significance of the loss. It was "disappointing" he wrote, in a stunning piece of understatement. The loss, he explained, was because "there are a number of exceptional factors in the form of corporate impairment losses and PPI costs, but we are also undergoing transformational restructuring as part of the outcome of our strategic review which is focused on enhancing the strength of our core bank."

Instead of recognising the scale of the loss as a serious trauma, it was presented as if it was a clearing of the decks for a tremendous move forward. The chair wrote: "As the business moves through this change and we concentrate on leveraging the strength of our brand in relationship banking services for both retail and business customers, I am confident that our continued focus on what is right for our customers and members will provide a strong platform for future growth."

That might now be regarded less as a statement of optimism, but rather of delusion. The impairment losses were bad enough in themselves, but in a sense the PPI losses were even more significant for an organisation that styled itself as the major British ethical bank. Despite this, Flowers commented: "Our continuing commitment to ethical banking, supporting our communities and 'doing the right thing' has never been more pertinent than today."

Despite the massive losses, the Bank was continuing to pursue the Verde deal. Barry Tootell was now the chief executive. In his statement in the financial report, Tootell wrote: "We believe the ethos of our business provides a solid platform to broaden our reach and appeal in the UK banking sector, whether that is through the Lloyd's deal (referred to as Project Verde) or through continued organic growth.

"Project Verde would see the equivalent of 10 years' growth in one business deal and the transaction would see us take a 7% market share of UK personal current accounts, with around 1,000 branches UK wide. We remain in active discussions with Lloyds Banking Group regarding the sale of its Verde business and both parties remain committed towards reaching an agreement. We have always been clear that any deal of this nature is complex and must satisfy the exacting interests of our customers and members."

Bye bye Verde

Despite the apparent and continued optimism within the Bank, The Co-operative Group's withdrawal from the purchase of 630 Lloyds Banking Group branches was not surprising. Several problems about the deal had surfaced and there had been growing anxiety behind the scenes. The banking operation would have trebled in size, but if the deal went badly wrong there was a recognition that it threatened more than just the banking side of the Group. One well-publicised problem was the need to strengthen the capital base of The Co-operative Banking Group. It had publicly suggested that the Lloyds deal would actually boost the Bank's capital position, because it came with capital from Lloyds. This seemed inexplicable and counter-intuitive.

A different story was published in the Financial Times. An additional £1bn was needed to satisfy regulators – previously the FSA, by now the PRA. In truth, behind the scenes the regulators were deeply sceptical about the Co-op's capacity to take over the Verde branch profile.

They were privately critical of the Bank's management capacity and quality. Regulators had concerns about the Bank as it stood, without taking on a massive expansion project. If it had not been for the perception that the Bank's bid was backed by senior political figures – in both major parties – the proposal may have been scuppered by regulators long before it ran out of steam.

Minutes, published much later, of meetings between the regulator and the Bank provide the real explanation for why Verde collapsed. The lead regulator at the FSA, Andrew Bailey (who went on to head up the PRA), had made clear that it did not believe the Co-op Bank was up to the job of taking over 632 Lloyds branches under Project Verde.

One of the big issues as far as the regulator was concerned was errors in the Bank's financial reporting and a mistake – to the Bank's advantage – in its reporting of its liquidity position. According to the minutes, Bailey "used the misreporting of the liquidity position to illustrate the deficiencies that existed in CFS's risk management. He said these were not acceptable and were indicative of weaknesses in the Group's broader risk management capacity and called into question its ability to entertain transactions such as Verde."

Without taking on Project Verde, the Bank needed to raise an extra £900m in capital, said the regulator. If it proceeded with Project Verde, it would need an extra £2bn. This had to be capital available to absorb losses, so the finance on offer from Lloyds itself to oil the wheels of the deal would not assist with this.

There had clearly been board rows about Verde. The FSA had approved Paul Flowers to be chair and requested that Rodney Baker-Bates – who had chaired Britannia since April 2008 – become board joint vice-chair. The arguments in their favour were that Flowers was perceived to be effective in his role at facilitating decisions, while Baker-Bates had a record inside and outside the financial services industry. He was a former Prudential UK chief executive and served on the boards of several banks. Baker-Bates resigned from the Bank's board in 2012 in protest at the decision to pursue Project Verde.

The FSA also 'requested' – an offer the Bank could not refuse – a second vice chair with direct financial services experience. This was David Davies – whose background was as a director of several insurance businesses, including as chief executive of Pearl Assurance. Davies also wanted to resign in 2012 because of his opposition to Project Verde. He was persuaded to delay his resignation to avoid the problems this would cause.

It is strange, to say the least, that the boards of the Bank and the Group did not at that point abort the Verde negotiations and accept this was an acquisition too far. For both vice chairs to express their wish to leave the board as they strongly disagreed with the core of their company's business strategy is unusual to say the least – yet there was little sign that the two boards recognised the significance of this. Nor is it obvious why the regulator did not take more assertive and interventionist action at this point.

Instead, options were considered by the Group to raise the necessary capital. One was disposal of the pharmacy business, which was suffering from low margins. Other disposals were discussed, as was the issuing of a members' bond. As far as the regulator was concerned, a preferred approach would have been for the Bank to improve its operational scale by merging with a European mutual bank, such as Rabobank. One senior Bank source privately told the author that while he would deny this in public, the Bank was willing in practice to consider this option.

But there had been serious tension, verging on animosity, between the Group chief executive, Peter Marks, and Neville Richardson. Richardson left his role as Bank chief executive by mutual agreement in July 2011, with a pay-off the Guardian reported was worth £4.6m, leaving Barry Tootell in charge. Richardson decided to go both because he believed Project Verde was a step too far and too fast, and because he could not accept a situation in which he reported to Marks.

Richardson agreed to go on 'gardening leave'. Anyway, he had a long-term plan to retire at 55 and was leaving only a short time before that. Despite this and the difficult situation the Bank was in, his pay-off was generous. It was less than two years after Richardson left that Verde collapsed under regulatory pressure. Regulators may have pulled the trigger, but there was relief in parts of the Bank and the Group. Peter Marks tried to put the best spin on the situation, making the announcement on behalf of the Group in April 2013. "After detailed and thorough consideration of all aspects of the Verde transaction, we have decided, at this time, that it is not in the best interests of our members to proceed with the transaction," he said.

Marks added: "The Verde transaction would not currently deliver a suitable return for our members within a reasonable time frame and with an acceptable level of risk ... we will continue to develop our Bank for the long-term, offering a real alternative on the high street with our strong, established brand and our reputation as a trusted financial services business."

There had been, however, a strategic peculiarity about Project Verde. The Co-op was to take on a large branch presence, in the face of an almost industry-wide desire to be rid of old fashioned bricks and mortar assets. While most traditional retail banks were closing branches, the Co-op saw its future in the past, through a massive branch network.

The aspiration was somehow symbolic of the wider co-op movement's response to progress – seeking comfort in the past and former ways of doing things. It was like the child who faces their fear of the future by holding onto their comfort blanket.

CHAPTER 6

Moody's Killer Blow

If the collapse of Project Verde seemed like bad news, worse was to come soon after. On 9th May 2013 the Moody's - one of the 'Big Three' credit agencies – delivered its verdict on the financial health of the Co-op Bank. It was a blow the Bank would never recover from. What happened in the following four and a half years was like watching a very slow-motion car crash.

Although the credibility of the credit ratings agencies was badly damaged by their failures to provide penetrating analyses of the capital instruments whose collapse triggered the credit crunch and global recession, adverse views from the agencies remained destructive to businesses' reputations and to the cost of their borrowing. So when Moody's – one of the largest agencies – issued a credit downgrade of the Bank in May 2013, it was very bad news indeed. This followed the announcement in March 2013 of the Bank's results and the £673.3m loss for the 2012 financial year.

Moody's comments on the Bank and CFS were damning. It was as if people in and around the Bank had been living in a dream, which Moody's suddenly pointed out was actually a nightmare. The Bank's problems, explained Moody's, went much deeper than the collapse of the Verde deal.

"While the abandonment of the deal is not a material driver of today's action, had it proceeded to completion the deal would have strengthened Co-operative Bank's franchise and increased its customer base," explained the agency. Moody's added that the deal would anyway have posed a number of challenges in terms of "capital, liquidity and execution risk".

Moody's judgement continued: "The lowering of the BCA [baseline credit assessment] reflects Moody's opinion that (1) the Bank faces the risk of further substantial losses in its non-core portfolio, as demonstrated recently by the unexpectedly significant deterioration of its commercial real estate (CRE) exposures, that will exert downward pressure on capital ratios that are already low relative to its peers; (2) its vulnerability to losses is heightened by the low level of provisions held against its lending portfolio; and (3) the Bank's slow progress in realising merger-related revenue and cost benefits has diminished its ability to replenish capital through earnings. Together, these imply a risk of write-downs on junior debt instruments and, potentially, the need for external support to maintain regulatory capital levels."

Moreover, Moody's warned that it might in the future cut the Bank's credit rating again. "The review for further downgrade will allow Moody's to examine the effectiveness of the Bank's plan to strengthen its capital structure, improve profitability and reduce its cost base once the full implications of the Prudential Regulatory Authority review are known by the Bank, which is not expected until end-May 2013," it said.

This was no snap decision by Moody's and was carefully argued. It followed what Moody's regarded as a "significant deterioration in the credit quality of the Bank's non-core portfolio" announced in its results in March 2013. This indicated that the losses exceeded the Bank's expectations and that earlier provisions for losses were inadequate. This, Moody's might have added, suggested serious financial management failures at the Bank.

"Most of these risks stem from the legacy portfolio of Britannia Building Society, which The Co-operative Bank acquired in 2009," the agency said. "Moody's believes that the Bank underestimated the risks of that acquisition, especially against the backdrop of the continued weak economic environment.

Moreover, the Bank's ability to generate the earnings needed to replenish capital, if higher losses materialise, is diminished by its slow progress in realising merger-related revenue and cost benefits."

The Bank's failure to achieve the efficiency savings that the merger was, in part, predicated upon was clearly a damning judgement by the agency. It summarised the case against the continuation of the Bank's former investment grade credit rating. Its capital levels were too low, it did not have sufficient cover for likely bad debts and it had limited capacity to generate profits.

Taken together this meant the Bank would have difficulty in absorbing likely future losses. As a result, those losses would probably fall on those who had loaned to the Bank through bond issues.

"Moody's believes that the combination of (1) low capital levels; (2) a low problem-loan coverage ratio relative to other UK banks; and (3) weak internal capital-generation capacity suggests that the Bank's capacity to absorb future losses is now too low to support an investment grade rating and that it possesses only speculative standalone strength, subject to high credit risk in the absence of extraordinary external support," added the agency. "The ratings assigned to the Bank's subordinated and junior subordinated debt reflect the possibility that losses may be imposed on holders of these securities in order to achieve the capitalisation levels that the UK regulators require."

The Bank goes into run-down

The bubble of inflated ego and self-congratulatory complacency that followed the takeover of the Britannia Building Society had been burst. Borrowing costs would rise. Even the terminology would make anyone shudder: the Bank's credit status had collapsed from 'prime' to 'junk'.

Moody's thought there were probably more nasty things hidden in the wood yard – otherwise known as the loan portfolio inherited from Britannia. And Moody's was right. What the Bank had decided was an excellent quality Britannia loan portfolio was actually junk. And because the decision was based on a lack of proper due diligence, the Bank had no one other than itself to blame.

A crisis was now enveloping The Co-operative Bank. It was not enough to breathe a sigh of relief that Verde had been abandoned; instead it was facing an existential crisis. The Bank was forced to accelerate the sale of non-core assets –

potentially crystallising losses on Britannia loan portfolios, such as non-performing buy-to-let mortgages. It also had to exit some business lines, particularly those where margins were low, which took up a lot of capital, or where turnover was too low to justify continued activity. It exited the markets for lending to housing associations and handling local authority accounts – both of which were niche markets where the Bank had enjoyed strong positions.

The Bank had been caught seriously by surprise by the scale and duration of the economic crisis. Even in 2011, its results reflected over-optimism in an economic recovery. Whether the Bank would have been in a stronger position to predict economic trends if – like most of its competitors – it had a senior economist is another interesting question. But economists, too, often get it wrong.

Major efforts to plug the hole in its finances included the disposal of its life assurance business, which was sold to Royal London in 2013. That raised more than £200m. The general insurance business was put up for sale, with hopes that this could generate £650m. While bids came in, these were significantly below the Bank's own valuation so the sale was aborted.

But once again, this sale and attempted sale raised questions about the Bank's strategy. A few years earlier it had embarked on an approach to cross-sell business between the Bank and insurance lines. That strategy had been approved despite the knowledge that the rest of the industry had abandoned bancassurance as futile.

The Bank had apparently thought it knew better than the rest of the industry – that its offer was sufficiently different as it was a 'manufacturer' of insurance products, not just a retailer of them – but it found in the end that it was not actually that different from the rest of the sector. Yet its assurance and insurance businesses were long-standing and many in the sector felt it was a shame to see one go and the other put up for sale.

Barry Tootell, at this point chief executive of the Bank, argued that the sale to Royal London now made sense. "We have a clear view of what is strategically important to ensure that the remarkable transformation of The Co-operative Group over the last five years is fully embedded and can be built upon," he said. "A part of this strategy is to focus on the Banking Group's core relationship retail and business banking operations ... This decision reflects changes in the life assurance market and our focus on developing a compelling co-operative offer for our millions of customers and members."

Another sting

If the volte-face on the insurance business was one admission of a major strategic failure, the write-down of £150m on the Project Finacle core-banking IT system announced in March 2013 was another.

The much-heralded Finacle was now aborted, all spending on it written off and recognised as a total waste of £349m. Not only that, but the Bank had to make provision for an additional £450m for a replacement IT system. Unlike Finacle, the newly commissioned system would support banking by smartphone – which by this time constituted around one in three banking transactions. Sir Christopher Kelly's review of the Bank's problems, published in April 2014, concluded that the collapse of the Finacle project stemmed from the changes in strategic direction that the Bank embarked upon over a few years.

The merger with Britannia had substantially increased the scope and complexity of the IT project. Sir Christopher believed that a high turnover of senior executives – in particular the loss of chief information officer Gerry Pennell, who had driven Project Finacle – caused considerable problems. Added to that were the cultural differences that had hindered the merger of Britannia and the Bank.

Sir Christopher's judgement was scathing. "The Bank's management seem to have underestimated the amount of work reconfiguration would entail both for [the contractor] Infosys and its own staff ... Continuing the replatforming programme while simultaneously attempting to integrate the two entities was itself very risky ... It is not unusual for quality assurance reviews to point out difficulties.

"The scale and consistency of the concerns raised about the Bank's replatforming programme is striking ... Key members of the programme leadership across different parts of the business did not enjoy functioning working relationships ... The programme team failed to push back hard enough against the business demand for amendments to Finacle.

"It gathered 18,000 requirements ... If the programme was ever to have had a chance of succeeding it would have had to have been robustly managed by people with the right capabilities and experience using the best possible project management discipline. It would also have had to be subject to searching challenge and scrutiny at board, executive and programme management levels. The Bank did not provide any of these things to the extent necessary to ensure success."

The failure of Project Finacle was itself a reflection of what had become a dysfunctional organisation. It failed because there was no coherent business strategy behind the Bank's operations and a sometimes poisonous relationship between key colleagues – with a division between those people who came from Britannia and those from the Bank, plus another division between those in the Bank and those in the Group. No wonder the Bank was in a mess.

And the figures get even worse

By the time the results were published in August 2013 of that year's interim trading performance, there could be no disguising the level of distress the Bank was in. The net half-year loss after tax was a staggering £781.5m. By then the Bank had a new chief executive – Niall Booker, formerly of HSBC – and a new chair, Richard Pym, who had been chair of the government's UK Asset Resolution operation. The scale of the Bank's crisis was such that in his report Pym went so far as to call the results "disappointing".

Auditors KPMG put it more bluntly. They warned there was "the existence of a material uncertainty which may cast significant doubt on the Bank's ability to continue as a going concern". To put this in simple language, without a viable rescue package, the Bank was potentially bust.

The main factor in the loss was a closer examination of what was contained in loan portfolios taken over from Britannia. This led to a write-down on their value of £496m. The Bank also had to write down the value of its IT by an additional £148.4m and set aside a further £25m for compensation for the mis-selling of PPI.

The largest element of the Bank's debtors was commercial property lending, much of which was high risk and loaned by Britannia. The second largest class of debtor was Private Finance Initiative schemes, to which the Bank loaned £1.25bn. Among other classes of borrowers to which large sums were loaned included renewable energy (£620m), the care sector (£317m), public sector entities (£173m) and education sector (£126m). The sectors in which there had been substantial levels of default were commercial investment (£1.3bn), hospitality (£259m) and residential investment (£131m), which were likely to be the result of lax lending practices at Britannia.

At this point the national media began looking at not just Britannia's past lending policies, but also those of the Bank. Its accounts showed that it was owed £34.4m from football clubs – which the Sunday Times reported constituted a loan to Celtic at a generous rate of 1.3%. In addition, a loan or loans had been issued to another club, or clubs, which was to the value of £15m and in default. Previously the Bank had lent to Derby County, Bolton Wonderers, Sheffield Wednesday, Coventry City, Stoke City and Manchester City.

The most controversial lending by the Bank was to the Labour Party, which in 2013 had a £1.2m loan outstanding, after borrowing several million pounds over the preceding years. According to records deposited with the Electoral Commission this was charged at a rate of 3.5% over base rate. Past substantial loans – £2.61m in 1999 and £2m in 2009 – were charged at rates of 2% and 3% over base rate. The money was hardly a gift at those rates – providing the debts were properly controlled and repaid on time. Loans from the Bank to some co-operative societies were being made in 2013 at little over 1%. The Labour Party also borrowed more than £1.2m from the Unity Trust Bank, which was at that time 26.66% owned by The Co-operative Bank (the balance owned by trades unions), charged at base rate plus 3.5%.

CHAPTER 7

Demutualisation

The massive losses announced by the Bank in March 2013 had to be borne by someone. Quite simply, the Bank did not have enough capital to absorb the losses, while also having capital reserves available in case things got even worse.

The solution was to raise new capital and eliminate some of the debt. New capital would be raised by issuing shares in the Bank, while some of the debt would be erased by converting it into equity. Both these measures meant, in effect, the partial demutualisation of the Bank.

Strictly speaking, the Bank had never been a mutual – it was a wholly owned plc subsidiary of a mutual. But that mutual – the Co-op Group – would no longer own the Bank, but rather have a stake in it. Despite this, it was agreed the 'Co-operative' name could stay providing the Group's stake did not fall below 20%, the Bank continued to abide by ethical principles, and it provided support to other co-operatives. While co-operative activists were disillusioned on seeing that the Bank's problems had led to a partial de-mutualisation, thousands of bondholders opposed the terms of the deal offered to them. Their loans would be converted into an ownership stake in a loss-making business.

Until that time, despite the Bank's problems, the bondholders had received a very good rate of return. Ten classes of debt securities that had been issued by the former Britannia Building Society or The Co-operative Bank were affected, with a total value of £1.3bn. Owners of this debt who were being paid fixed rates were receiving between 5.75% and 9.25% – very high rates by 2013, given the prevailing economic climate. Some other bondholders were tied into floating rates that were less generous.

The Bank claimed that about 7,000 individual investors were affected, but Mark Taber of Fixed Income Investments – who represented many of them – said the correct figure was around 15,000 individuals. The numerical difference, suggested Taber, was the large number of individuals holding bonds through nominee accounts. "These [bonds] were always popular with pensioners for income and with retail investors," Taber said at the time.

"Many people have held these investments since the 1990s and are not capable of keeping in touch with what is happening. Many are in old people's homes." Some of these, he added, needed the bond interest payments to meet their residential care costs.

Not surprisingly, many of the individual bondholders were willing to sell. So, too, were some of the institutional investors. It is thought that this included some of the UK's best-known insurers, but these made sure to keep their heads down and avoid publicity around investing in what had become a failed company.

But this is where things became 'interesting' – as in the Chinese curse, 'may you live in interesting times'. These were indeed 'interesting times' and they were a curse on the co-operative movement. The hedge funds moved in.

The two leading funds that swam against the tide by positively deciding to buy debt in The Co-operative Bank were Aurelius Capital and Silver Point. It was rumoured each had bought bonds at a small proportion of their face value.

Aurelius Capital is based in New York and acquired a substantial amount of the Bank's lower tier two debt. The purchases were from institutional investors who no longer wanted to hold the debt. Aurelius is a $2.5bn (£1.6bn) fund that has a reputation for buying distressed debt cheaply and then aggressively improving its value, by playing hardball in negotiations.

Aurelius was particularly successful in doing so with Dubai World – a Middle East investment vehicle that was badly damaged by the global financial crisis. After a tough stand-off with negotiators, Aurelius doubled the value of its stake in Dubai World. While all other creditors accepted an offer of 50 cents in the dollar, Aurelius rejected the proposal and stuck to its demand for full value restitution. Eventually, according to reports, Aurelius was bought out at near to par value by a party close to Dubai World.

Elsewhere, Aurelius was one of the bondholders – after acquiring the distressed debt cheaply, probably at 20% of face value – in Anglo Irish Bank, which was rescued by the Irish government at enormous cost to the country's taxpayers. As well as holding an investment itself, Aurelius represented two other funds that bought into the debt.

Aurelius was also involved in heavy negotiations with the Greek government, after buying distressed sovereign debt.

The fund was blamed for delaying resolution of a big US company – the Chicago Tribune – in its attempt to come out of protective bankruptcy when Aurelius tried to maximise the value of the debt it is holding.

The biggest investment by Aurelius is thought to be in Argentinian government debt, which has become the subject of legal action in the international courts. Argentina reneged on much of its sovereign debt, claiming that it was effectively bankrupt. In 2005, the country replaced old debt instruments with new debt that was heavily discounted. While most creditors accepted the offer, Aurelius – having bought the debt at a large discount – refused. Aurelius was willing to be patient – its legal dispute with Argentina made slow progress through the courts. Its reward was reportedly around three quarters of a billion dollars in profit when the government eventually paid up.

In short, Aurelius is an example of what is sometimes called a 'vulture fund', which takes on debt that appears to have little or no value – and then takes aggressive legal action to maximise the value of that debt. It is willing to do this in the face of pleas that the legal action jeopardises a course of action agreed with most of the creditors.

Silver Point Capital, which also bought up a large quantity of distressed debt held in the Co-op Bank, adopts a similar approach to Aurelius. But with more than $8bn (£5.3bn) in assets under ownership, it is significantly bigger than Aurelius and is listed as one of the US's 100 largest hedge funds. It was established in 2002 by two former Goldman Sachs bankers, who both had strong reputations for their handling of distressed debt.

Like Aurelius, Silver Point has a record of willingness to negotiate hard for its interests and for using the law aggressively. However, its distressed debt purchases have often been motivated by seeing opportunities for improved value in the underlying asset, rather than scrapping over the spoils of a dead business or bankrupt country.

According to some media reports, Aurelius and Silver Point between them now owned the majority of certain classes of debt in the Co-op Bank. This gave them a very strong negotiating position, along with another six investment funds that owned bonds that were being represented by Moelis.

The more numerous individual retail investors had much less capital invested, around £65m in total, and many of them had invested in the Bank to express support for the movement. Mark Taber, representing thousands of those retail investors, told the author at the time that he was unsurprised by the activities of Aurelius and Silver Point. "They are hedge funds – and that is what hedge funds do with banks that are distressed," he said.

Taber added that he believed the PRA and its predecessor the FSA should take responsibility for making the crisis worse in their failure to provide earlier warning of the capital weakness of the Bank. He also claimed that the PRA had allowed a "false market" to operate in the Bank's bonds by the failing to disclose its knowledge of the calamitous state of the Bank.

The Bank and its advisors were aware that hedge funds were buying into its debt as soon as there were indications of serious difficulty in March 2013. By then there were three interest groups among the holders of Bank debt.

Small investors were looking for either cash recompense, or the reinstatement of dividend payments, in full and as soon as possible. Institutional investors that had held onto their debts were looking to maximise value and were willing to invest for the long term if they were persuaded by the Bank's prospectus. The third group of investors was the hedge funds, whose commitment was to show a return against the price at which they bought the debt. That could be achieved either through litigation that forced the Bank to buy back the debt at face value, or near to it, or else by forcing the market price of the debt to rise and then selling on the bonds.

After weeks of pressure, the Co-op Group entered into negotiations with the bondholders to resolve what had become an impasse over the restructuring of the Bank. Some of the bondholders demanded that the Group be left with zero equity.

The negotiations had been the result of a significant shift in attitude at the Group. Initially, requests by bondholders to meet with the Bank were rejected. Bondholders complained they were given a response that was akin to 'take it or leave it' – the 'it' being detailed proposals to be revealed in the prospectus. At this point the Group expected to lodge an additional £500m of capital in the Bank by selling both the life assurance and the general insurance businesses.

But bondholders were angry and demanded to meet with the Bank and Group. Swiss bank UBS was advising the Bank and Group and began to meet the bondholders' representatives Moelis on a regular basis. The objective by now was to ensure the prospectus was acceptable to the hedge funds and other classes of bondholders.

While the PRA was attempting to be hands-off in its approach to the crisis at the Bank, it did let it be known that it would resist an attempt by the hedge funds to take control of the Bank and insert a new management team without experience of running a UK bank. However, one private equity firm – JC Flowers – had gained relevant experience through its takeover via the Butterfill Act of the Kent Reliance Building Society and was rumoured to be keen to be involved. That interest, though, never converted into active engagement in the project.

By this time, institutional investors were holding the dominant hand, owning between them about 70% of equity in the new business through the potential conversion of debt into equity. The Group would be left as a minority shareholder, owning just 30% of the equity – the same as the vulture funds, but less than all the institutional shareholders collectively.

The Bank published the agreement it reached with bondholders, describing it as "the Terms of a Capital Raising Plan to Secure the Long Term Future of the UK's Leading Ethical Bank". This would raise about £700m of additional tier one (loss bearing) capital, positioning it to "meet regulatory capital requirements in full in the medium term". The arrangement was approved by the PRA. As well as converting much of the debt into equity, it also enabled cash to be paid to certain retail investors to buy them out.

CHAPTER 8

The Directors

While the Bank approached its restructuring – partial demutualisation – there were significant changes at executive and non-executive level at the Bank and The Co-operative Group.

Group chair Len Wardle stepped down from the Bank's board. Duncan Bowdler, Peter Harvey and Bob Newton all resigned as non-executive directors. The only remaining Bank directors without experience at a senior level of the industry were the new Group CEO Euan Sutherland (who replaced Peter Marks in April 2013) and Ben Reid, CEO of Midcounties Co-op. (Reid, it should be noted, was widely considered to have had a difficult relationship with Marks.)

The changes at the Bank's board level were reported to be the result of the demands from the institutional investors and were acceptable to the PRA. The big reduction in Group influence effectively reversed Project Unity, which had aimed to bring the Group and the Bank closer together. At executive level, there were also widespread changes. Deputy chief executive Rod Bulmer left, despite urgings that he stayed. The departure of Barry Tootell as chief executive was not regretted. Niall Booker – whose background included a long period with HSBC – took over as chief executive. His role initially included being deputy chief executive of the Group, but that responsibility was soon dropped as the two entities continued to separate.

Treasury Select Committee hearings

Differing explanations for the reasons for the crisis at the Bank were presented to the House of Commons Treasury Select Committee, which held an investigation into the Bank and its attempted acquisition of the Lloyds TSB branches through Project Verde.

Neville Richardson gave evidence to the Treasury Select Committee in which he questioned whether the relationship between the Bank and the Group had been appropriate. Richardson was particularly critical of Project Unity – one of Marks' pet ideas.

"During 2010 I became increasingly concerned at Co-op Group's aim to fully integrate CFS within Co-op Group from a management and administrative point of view," said Richardson in his written evidence to the committee. "I made my concerns that this would cause serious disruption and distraction to the CFS business known to Len Wardle (Group chair) and Paul Flowers (CFS chair) on a number of occasions. I felt that the agenda was being driven from Group, and by Peter Marks in particular. It was not taking into account the risks which would be created in the Bank.

I expressed my concerns to Peter Marks directly in April 2010, when he first told me that Project Unity was going to take place in 2011. I also expressed these concerns to Paul Flowers and Len Wardle at the Annual Board offsite in July 2010 and at a dinner between the three of us in June/July 2010. I believed that the disruption at a time when the Britannia merger was not complete and the IT systems replacement was in progress was highly dangerous. I sat on the Project Unity steering committee and frequently made my concerns over timing and potential disruption to the bank known.

"The integration commenced in early 2011. My reporting line changed from the Chairman and Board of CFS to Peter Marks. Project Unity gathered pace and it became apparent it would involve transferring responsibility for key bank activities including finance, strategy, HR, communications, governance, legal and internal audit to Group control."

Giving his evidence to the House of Commons Treasury Select Committee, Peter Marks seemed to suggest the Bank's crisis was, if not an act of God, at least the result of a situation that could not have been anticipated or prevented. "I guess it was a victim of the economy," he said. "The loans that were made in Britannia have gone sour to some extent because of the economy. We should remember that banks need to be able to compete; they need scale. That was the strategy behind the Britannia deal. I repeat that I was not driving the Britannia deal, but as a non-executive director I voted for it when it was proposed." He added in later testimony: "I still think, looking back, that strategically, the Britannia merger was the right thing to do."

Marks continued: "We hired consultants – advisers – to do proper due diligence. It was a lengthy process and fair value was attached to the assets of the business. We accepted the advice that we were given ... As a non-executive director of the Bank, of course I share responsibility. Should we have merged with Britannia Building Society? If we had had a crystal ball, of course we wouldn't have, but we relied very heavily on the fair value and due diligence work that was done on our behalf."

Marks also argued that the collapse of the Bank could be regarded positively for the Group as a whole. "It is a tragedy, but in many ways it can be seen as a good thing," he said. "In actual fact, it will force the Co-op to focus on fewer businesses and not stretch its capital in the way it has done."

MPs questioned whether the root cause had been the lack of due diligence undertaken by and for the Bank prior to its takeover of Britannia. "How much due diligence did you do?", Marks was asked by Mark Garnier MP. "An enormous amount," he replied. The Bank had asked its auditors KPMG to do due diligence; the firm issued a statement suggesting that the level of due diligence was not "an enormous amount". Instead it said: "KPMG conducted some due diligence ahead of the Britannia deal. We did not, however, undertake any due diligence on the corporate loan book. Our due diligence work did not include a recommendation on the merits of the Britannia deal."

Marks was not only Group chief executive for much of the period in question, but also chair of the Group's risk committee. With the benefit of hindsight, it might be concluded that this was an unwise combination of roles.

There was a contradiction at the heart of the Bank's operations that were not fully explored when it should have been. For the Group, the Bank's profits were large and an important contribution to overall Group profitability. But the return on capital by the Bank was not actually as large as it should have been, compared to other banks and building societies.

Profits as a percentage of income seem to have been very low for the industry – in most years it was 0.8%, or thereabouts. Comparing this with other financial services businesses is very difficult. There are inconsistencies in how income is reported between different types of provider and no other financial services provider has a strictly comparable business model.

My impression was that profits were probably around half the level that they should have been for this type and size of business. Credit ratings agencies probably also paid too little attention to the Bank's financial reports – a process anyway made difficult because the Bank's reports were less transparent than they should have been.

Another way to examine the profit base of the Bank is to look at its cost/income ratio. All of the main commercial banks in the year 2012 had a cost/income ratio of around 60%. For Lloyds, it was under 60%, HSBC a bit over that and Barclays a bit higher again. Even the trouble-hit RBS managed just over 60%. A year later, its crisis-hit Ulster Bank division reported a cost/income ratio of 61% – which it said was far too high and has been a driver for a substantial branch closure programme.

The industry has been heavily focused in recent years on bringing down the cost/income ratio. In 2008, the cost/income ratio at Yorkshire Building Society was 73%, but more recently it has been pulled down to one of the lowest in the sector, at 54%. Meanwhile, the Nationwide cut its cost/income ratio to its best ever level of 54.8% in 2013. So how did The Co-operative Bank compare? Badly, in simple terms. In 2011 the cost/income ratio was 66%, then in 2012 it rose to 74% and in 2013 it hit 85%. Northern Rock was the pioneer in low cost/income ratios – its collapse came about from low margins and dependency on wholesale markets, which seized in the early days of the credit crunch, not because of its drive to cut costs. Northern Rock's cost/income ratio was a bit above 30%, at a time when the industry standard was about 40%.

So, we can see that The Co-operative Bank was probably about twice where it should have been in terms of its costs when compared to income. (Profit is not everything, but without sufficient profit to build reserves and allocate investment a bank is basically stuffed.) Even allowing for the skewing effect of the Great Recession, the Bank's cost income ratio is about 25% to 30% above where it should be, if we take the Nationwide and the big clearing banks as benchmarks.

One of the significant factors behind these figures is what happened after the merger with Britannia. Part of the rationale was to achieve economies of scale, to bring down costs per customer – in other words, the cost/income ratio. Instead, no such thing happened. The Kelly report was highly critical on this, pointing out that the necessary decisions were not taken, that the economies of scale to be achieved by the merger were not achieved, that the executives and non-executives did not get on with the job. Perhaps they were simply preoccupied with all the other things going on. But they should not have been.

CHAPTER 9

The End Game

The restructuring of the Bank following the bad results in 2013 was not sufficient to resolve its underlying problems. This was essentially a lack of underlying profit during a prolonged period of general economic weakness, which was followed by ongoing low interest rates. That lack of profit meant the Bank was unable to strengthen its capital buffers from its own operations.

Meanwhile, it was being penalised by regulators over breaches in its sale of PPI policies and it was selling non-core assets to focus on core banking activities. In doing so, it was weakening its own capital position.

This reached a new crisis in early 2017. The Bank announced it was at serious risk of breaching the capital buffers it had agreed with the PRA. The Bank was still meeting the minimum capital target it set for itself – 10% common equity tier 1 (CET1) – which was an important measure of its financial strength and some way above the normal industry regulatory requirement of 6%. However, it expected this to fall below the agreed level in the following months. In a statement to investors, it said: "The Bank is updating its previous guidance and now expects its CET1 ratio will fall and remain below 10% over the medium term and that it is unlikely to meet its individual capital guidance over the planning period to 2020."

Negative media coverage speculated that the PRA would tell the Bank that it must strengthen its capital position. This created a difficulty for the investors, who were not keen to throw good money after bad. Moreover, one of those that had invested – Perry Capital – was now in wind-down mode.

The Co-op Group remained an owner of a minority stake in the Bank but had no appetite – or ready capital – to invest in it. Rather, its continued equity ownership was still damaging the Group's financial position. In its interim results statement for 2016, the Group announced it had written down the value of its stake in the Bank from £185m to £140m, generating a loss of £45m. This, said the Group in its accounts, is "consistent with falls in bank valuations generally".

Fitch Ratings, another of the 'Big Three' credit agencies, responded to the Bank's announcement on its capital position with a detailed analysis. The Bank's guidance, said Fitch, "highlights the difficulty of turning around troubled UK banks, particularly while interest rates remain low and the economic outlook remains uncertain".

But Fitch recognised that the Co-op Bank faced specific challenges in its trading position. "Co-op Bank, in particular, is struggling to return to profitability as it is focusing on residential and buy-to-let mortgage lending, where yields are generally tight," said Fitch. "The base rate cut in August 2016 is likely to have hit the Bank's revenue generation plans, as a large portion of its legacy loan book is sensitive to falling rates. At the same time, Co-op Bank is incurring high costs to enhance its systems and procedures to increase efficiency and improve risk controls."

Fitch believed the Bank's relaunch was "crucial" for it to become a viable business, but recognised that losses and capital erosion continued to hamper its progress. "We expect Co-op Bank to report losses until at least 2017," it said, "and significant investment in new systems could extend losses into the medium term. Profitability should begin to benefit in 2018 when fair value adjustments related to the 2009 acquisition of Britannia Building Society are fully unwound."

It added: "a return to structural profitability depends on Co-op Bank's ability to generate new, better-quality and higher-yielding mortgage loans and to reduce operating costs, particularly through improved automation and digitalisation."

Yet Fitch continued to assess the Bank's funding and liquidity positions as "relatively sound", with funds available from customer deposits and access to additional sources of finance. "We believe the Bank will maintain sufficient capital to remain viable," it said, "but its margin of safety is limited and a material weakening of the economic environment could lead us to question the viability of its business model."

The markets were more concerned. Following the Bank's statement on its capital position, the value of some of its bonds fell by 30%. This reflected a growing fear that the bonds could end up completely written off as part of a government rescue or other emergency restructuring.

CHAPTER 10

The End Of The Road?

In early 2017, it seemed as if the end of the road was near for The Co-operative Bank as an independent business. Turning round a loss-making bank is very difficult. Progress had been made, but it was time to see if there was an appetite in the market to buy the Bank and it put itself up for sale. There were rumours that potential bidders included Virgin Money, Clydesdale, JC Flowers, Santander and the now-sold TSB group. (TSB was initially separated from Lloyds through a share listing, before being bought by the Spanish Sabadell bank in 2017).

The notice of sale of the Bank was announced on 13 February 2017. Liam Coleman, by now the latest chief executive, explained: "Since 2013, we have successfully addressed significant legacy issues, reduced the cost base and rebuilt our franchise and customer proposition. The Co-operative Bank delivers an attractive banking proposition that is differentiated by our values and ethics and is highly valued by our four million customers. Customers value The Co-operative Bank and our ethical brand is a point of difference that sets us apart in the market.

"While our plan has been impacted by lower for longer interest rates, the costs associated with the sheer scale of the transformation and the legacy issues we faced in 2013, there is considerable potential to build the Bank's retail franchise further using the strength of the brand, its reputation for strong customer service and distinctive ethical position."

Consequently, said the Bank: "The Board is commencing a sale process, something always considered a potential outcome of the turnaround plan, alongside considering other options to build capital and meet the longer term capital requirements applicable to all UK banks... The cost base has reduced by over 20% since 2014, well over half of the original non-core portfolio has been sold, critical IT improvements have been delivered, risk management and operational resilience have improved substantially and the major legacy issues of the past, including customer remediation and PPI, have largely been addressed. Importantly, there is clear evidence of strong and sustained customer demand for the Bank's ethically led UK retail banking proposition, which has four million customers.

"The Bank has always been clear that, although it meets its Pillar 1 regulatory capital requirements and expects to continue to do so, it needs to build its capital and meet longer term UK bank regulatory capital requirements. Its capacity to do so organically has been constrained by the impact of interest rates that are lower than previously forecast, reducing the Bank's ability to generate income, and by higher than anticipated transformation and conduct remediation costs. The Bank has also needed to consider enhanced regulatory capital requirements expected of all UK banks...

"As a result, and having concluded its annual planning review, the Board is today commencing a sale process, inviting offers for all of the issued ordinary share capital of the Bank, and is also considering ways to raise equity capital from existing and new capital providers and a potential liability management exercise of its outstanding public debt."

However, none of the rival banks submitted an acceptable bid – and rumours suggested none put in any bid for the entire Bank. There was interest in splitting the Bank up, but how far these negotiations went is unclear since the sale process was abandoned. With the Bank no longer for sale, institutional bondholders agreed to transfer more debt into equity. They provided additional funds to meet regulatory capital requirements. The Co-operative Group's 20% stake – by now written off by the Group as of nil value – fell to just 1%. The Bank retained the right to the brand name, despite ceasing to be in any sense a co-operative enterprise.

Through this latest deal, £700m of additional tier one capital would be reported by the Bank. This comprised £250m of new equity, plus around £443m of recapitalisation through institutions' bonds being converted to shares. Smaller investors – those holding less than £100,000 each – would be given cash at a rate of 45 pence per £1 held in bonds. The arrangement was approved by the Prudential Regulation Authority.

A sticking point hampering negotiations was the treatment of pension liabilities. Historically the Bank had been part of the Group's pension scheme. The Bank's pension liabilities – which increased significantly through the takeover of Britannia Building Society – had to be separated from those of the Group. But calculating which entity had which assets and which liabilities was a complex process, which took several months to assess and negotiate. Pension scheme trustees, the Group and the Bank eventually agreed how to split the pension fund's assets and liabilities, with separate pension schemes being established for the Group and Bank. Around 21% of the joint scheme's assets and liabilities would go to the Bank's pension scheme.

This arrangement left the Bank's pension scheme in deficit. To address this, it was agreed that the Bank would contribute £100m over the following decade. The Bank would provide this through annual payments of £12.5m per year for five years and £7.5m for the following five years. It also agreed to provide upfront collateral for the pension scheme of £216m at the point of separation for the two schemes. This arrangement appeared not to have any negative implication for the Group's balance sheet. However, if the Bank's pension scheme performs badly, there could be a subsequent call on the Group for additional contributions.

In a statement, the Group said the deal provided assurance for the Bank's long-term future, including "agreement on the future structure of the shared Co-operative Pension Scheme ... [this] provides security for scheme members".

The Bank's stated commitment to ethical values is unaffected by its separation from the Group.

Bank chair Dennis Holt said: "The board is pleased to confirm this proposal for a recapitalisation which will mean The Co-operative Bank can continue as a viable stand-alone entity, with values and ethics at its heart. It is a great outcome for our customers. Our investors share our commitment to building our distinctive ethical franchise and see strong future growth potential for The Co-operative Bank."

Liam Coleman was quoted by the Financial Times as saying: "Our ambition is to return the Bank to full capital strength and safeguard our ethical franchise."

Institutional investors responded by forming themselves into an 'ad hoc committee', or AHC. A representative of these investors said: "We have supported the turnaround of The Co-operative Bank since 2013 and this further investment will provide the Bank with the capital needed to realise its potential as the UK's leading ethical bank." Aurelius having sold its stake, those institutional investors were led by the remaining hedge funds, which the Bank named as Silver Point Capital, GoldenTree Asset Management, Anchorage Capital Group, Blue Mountain Capital Management and Cyrus Capital.

The Bank's core attractions were still threefold: its ethical positioning; the steadfast loyalty of a large customer base; and the name. But each of those marketing advantages also had a risk attached.

Triodos Bank had established a trusted reputation as a bank offering accounts to charities and it launched itself as an ethical retail bank, with the explicit objective of taking customers away from the Co-op Bank. This threatened to undermine the loyalty of those four million customers, who were perhaps motivated by the continued use of the Co-operative name.

But with almost no structural connection with the traditional co-operative movement – and with no element of truly mutual ownership – was it really possible for The Co-operative Bank to use a name that was fundamentally misleading and arguably untrue? Is it enough for a bank to eschew the worst excesses of capitalism and to promise to make payments to new co-operative ventures for it to retain the name The Co-operative Bank? That may one day be a decision for the government, and for whoever is then the secretary of state with responsibility for business to decide.

But co-operative purists will be certain in their minds of the outcome. Through a process of neglect, negligence, hubris and the over-promotion of people with inadequate capabilities, an important institution had collapsed. The UK's original ethical bank had fallen and would not be reborn.

Conclusion: What do we learn?

The Co-operative Bank continues. Or at least that is what the television advertisements say – and still with the commitment to ethical values. But it is a very different Co-operative Bank in terms of ownership. The Co-operative Group no longer has even a minority stake in the Bank. And while the Bank retains the 'Co-operative' name, this is clearly a misnomer. It is a bank that was formerly owned by a co-op and which still promises to provide support to co-operative businesses and to act ethically. That may be good – despite the hedge fund ownership – but it is not a co-operative in any reasonable understanding of the word.

If anyone doubts this, ask the simple question – where will the profits (if there are any) go with the restructured Co-op Bank? When it was wholly owned by The Co-operative Group, the profits went to the Group, were reinvested, strengthened the Group, brought prices down and some of the time went as dividends to customers of the Group. Under the new structure, eventually the profits will go again as dividends – but this time, to the equity owners of the hedge fund investors. That is no co-operative.

So where did it go wrong? The answer is not simple. In the terms of a Greek tragedy, it is hubris and nemesis. Decision-makers believed their own hype and got it wrong. But who were those decision-makers? It was the executives – of the Group, the Bank and the Britannia. It was also the board members of those same organisations. Plus the regulators. And even the government – Gordon Brown's boast of having overcome the old boom-and-bust cycles comes to mind. There is no clearer example of hubris and nemesis than that.

Another example of hubris was when David Anderson, while chief executive of the Bank, claimed that it had avoided the mistakes of the majority of the banking sector and had emerged from the global financial crisis in strong shape. He was wrong, even before the Bank took over Britannia.

While the Bank looked in good shape, its costs were actually too high compared to its income. One of the effects of this was that it was in a bad position to ride out difficult times. This was especially true as the Bank had been mis-selling PPI for years. Compensation costs for that mis-selling were to be a drag on the financial results for years to come, making a loss making situation much worse. Moreover, an ethical bank should not have been in the situation of selling insurance policies that were not suited to the needs of their customers. That feels like a skin-deep ethical policy.

Then there was the issue of the IT system. Writing off ill-advised IT investments and then creating provisions to procure replacement kit was another key factor in the Bank's financial crisis. But that was much more than a failure in IT procurement policy. True, there were serious problems with the system that was bought. But many of the weaknesses resulted from confused and inconsistent business strategies.

Again, the hubris is evident – executives and boards believed that they could go in the opposite direction to the rest of the finance industry: using IT systems and customer loyalty to cross-sell banking and insurance products (the bancassurance model). While the big banks and insurers were giving up on this model, the Co-op Bank pursued it enthusiastically. Unsurprisingly, it met with failure too.

That, though, was not the only strategic business failure. Just as significant was the volte-face on the direction of the business, which saw the Bank jump at the chance to take over Britannia just as the commitment to bancassurance was being implemented.

Nor was this a one-off. It had already considered the purchase of Norwich & Peterborough Building Society, where it concluded the business was not in good enough shape to be bought. So having decided that expansion lay in selling more insurance products, it then decided the best opportunity lay in increasing mortgage lending through a merger with a building society. Even though that meant that the IT investment was now a waste. Bizarre.

My interpretation of these events is that the strategy was not fully thought through. There was only superficial commitment to one business model, when suddenly another one came along. Blame for that lies with those executives who put forward the strategies, and with the board members who went along with it.

Here, I disagree with Myners' review, which placed disproportionate blame on the boards. A succession of executives at both the Group and the Bank cannot walk away from responsibility that easily, especially as they formulated the strategies that the boards accepted.

But there is another dimension here, too. Having rejected the possibility of taking over the Norwich & Peterborough Building Society, why on earth did the Co-op Bank not also walk away from Britannia? The regulator – at that point the Financial Services Authority – regarded the deal as a rescue, though apparently keeping that view to itself. Why did the Bank believe otherwise?

The key to this is the failure of the Bank to do the proper due diligence. The reason for this, at least in part, was the ostensible desire of the Britannia to keep secret the negotiations for the merger.

It apparently told the Bank that there could be no due diligence that involved physically accessing the Britannia's offices. As a result, all the books that should have revealed the building society's potential black holes remained closed to the Bank until much later, by which time it was too late. But even that might not have been a disaster. Even with a weak Britannia, the deal could have worked. To do so, the merger would have been followed by a rigorous cost-cutting exercise, improving the cost-income ratio and rationalising the business. Yet the merged business was led by the former chief executive of Britannia, who did not achieve – or apparently even seriously attempt – cost cutting.

There is certainly an argument that an ethical business should treat staff well and avoid job losses – but not at the expense of the business losing its viability and sustainability. That, as Moody's credit agency later pointed out, was exactly what happened.

It might be thought on the basis of this analysis that perhaps the Bank failed simply because it was 'too nice' to be viable – 'too nice' to take the tough decisions. Yet no one ever accused the Group chief executive who drove the change process, Peter Marks, of being 'too nice' to take tough decisions. Nor was the accusation made against Neville Richardson, who was first chief executive of Britannia and then – also bizarrely – chief executive of the Co-op Bank.

A more likely explanation is overreach. Both the Group and the Bank tried to do too many things, with the result that strategic objectives became swamped by day-to-day necessities. The strategy fell victim to daily management. And the board failed to demand the change process that it should have overseen.

But overreach is also another way of describing hubris and nemesis, or believing your own hype. This can be thought of as powerful figures imposing on the business their personal legacy. We all want to be remembered. And in business it is so much better to be remembered as the person who 'saved the Co-operative Group' or 'built the modern Co-operative Bank', than as the person who almost destroyed the retail co-operative movement and let the bank exit the co-operative sector.

And the reality is that some key decision-makers acted as if their desire to have a legacy that recognised their central role in rebuilding the movement was the most important thing. So important that for their own footnote in history they risked the largest co-operative retail society and destroyed its bank.

This is not to say that only the executives were to blame and the boards were blameless. And the boards of the Group, Bank and Britannia should have been stronger, more decisive, more assertive – and more skilled. They failed to hold executives to account. But it is also recognised that were too often kept in the dark. News of the Britannia merger came via the media as far as Bank board members were concerned. There can be no clearer sign of the breakdown of relationships between the executives and board than that silence.

So when the House of Commons Treasury Select Committee made clear its disdain for Paul Flowers and his lack of knowledge of banking, we should reflect on a few points. Firstly, his alleged use of drugs is not obviously relevant to his ability to be chair of a bank. Secondly, and more significantly, he was not the chair of the Bank when it made its fateful decision to take over the Britannia and to appoint the chief executive of a failing institution of the successor Bank. Paul Flowers was not a good chair of The Co-operative Bank, but he was not the reason the Bank failed.

There were clear systemic problems at the heart of The Co-operative Bank, and the failures were in both strategy and execution, at board-level in the Group, the Bank and within Britannia.

They were exacerbated by comparable failings by the regulator and arguably within government, for neglecting to ensure banks were regulated more stringently so that they could have survived the global financial crisis in good shape. But most of all, it was a failure of greed. Not perhaps for personal wealth – though some of the executives and board members did pretty well from their pay, bonuses and expense accounts. But another form of greed – the greed of demanding that personal ambitions were given priority.

And that is itself a sin – the form of business that is supposed to support the common good was brought down by people who put their own reputations first.

It has to be hoped that other co-operatives learn the lesson that greed and co-operation are not compatible.

INDEX

Acheson, Alex, 8
Alderson, Keith, 41-42
Anchorage Capital Group, 95
Anderson, David, 26, 34
Anglo Irish Bank, 73
Aurelius Capital, 73-77, 95

Bailey, Andrew, 34, 37, 55-56
Baker-Bates, Rodney, 56
bancassurer model, 26-27, 28, 65, 98
Bank of England Prudential Regulatory Authority, 32, 38-42, 55-56, 75, 76-77, 87-88
banking industry
    bad takeover decisions, 23
    bancassurer model, 26-27, 28, 65, 98
    comparison of banks, 82-84
    economic cycles, 25
    financial crash, 33
    trend away from branches, 33, 46, 50-51, 58
Barclays Bank, 83
Bennett, Graham, 26
Blue Mountain Capital Management, 95
Booker, Niall, 68, 80
Britannia Building Society
    Capital Investment Group subsidiary, 30
    Co-operative Bank merger, 20, 23-35, 63, 64, 65
    Illius subsidiary, 30
    loans and mortgages, 33, 40, 64, 68-69, 81
    merger benefits, 28-29, 31, 34, 84

Britannia Building Society (*continued*)
    merger due diligence, 29-35, 40, 81-82, 99, 101
    merger effects on Lloyds TSB purchase, 49
    merger problems, 29-35, 66-67, 68-69, 72, 81, 84, 89
    pension liability, 94
    regulator's concerns and warnings, 30, 34-35, 37-38
    selling of insurance products, 28
building societies
    and Co-operative Bank, 25-26, 51, 98, 99
    legislation, 23-25, 77
    (*See also* Britannia Building Society.)
Bulmer, Rod, 80
Burlton, Bob, 35
Butterfill, John and Butterfill Act, 23-25, 77

Chicago Tribune, 74
Coleman, Liam, 95
Co-operative Bank
    banking and insurance integration, 26-27, 28, 50, 51, 65-68, 98
    board changes, 79-84
    board's role in attempted purchase of Lloyd's branches, 48-52, 56
    board's role in decision making, 9, 26, 27, 28, 29, 32, 35, 41, 97-101
    bonds and bond holders, 63, 72, 76, 93
    branches, 33, 46, 50-51, 58
    Britannia merger, 23-35, 63, 64, 65, 66-67, 68-69, 72, 81, 84, 89
    Britannia merger due diligence, 29-35, 40, 81-82, 99, 101
    building societies proposed absorption, 25-26, 51, 98, 99
    capital strength, 37, 39, 46, 55, 56, 62, 71, 75, 87-89, 92-93, 95, 97
    control framework, 38, 51
    Co-operative Bank name following
    demutualisation, 71, 93, 95-96
    credit downgrade, 61-66
    culture, 40-41, 67-68
    customer service, 7-8
    demutualisation, 71-77, 91-93, 95-96
    description in notice of sale, 91-93
    ethical policy, 7, 8-9, 52, 92, 94, 95, 96, 99

Co-operative Bank (*continued*)
    European mutual bank possible merger, 57
    expansion policy, 25, 46, 50, 51, 54, 58, 81, 84
    financial crash effects, 33
    financial crisis, 52-58, 65
    financial misreporting, 37-42
    governance, 9, 26, 27, 28, 29, 32, 35, 41, 48-52, 56, 79-84
    hedge funds involvement, 72-77, 95, 96
    housing association and local authority business, 65
    internet banking capability, 28
    Kelly Review, 30-31, 66-67, 84
    Lloyds branches customers, 49
    management and board roles in strategy development, 9, 26, 27, 28, 32, 97
    management failures, 63, 67-68, 69, 97-101
    mortgages and loans, 28, 50, 68-69
    ownership, 11, 57, 71-77, 88, 91-97
    Payment Protection Insurance, 53, 68, 87, 92, 97
    penalties imposed by regulators, 41, 42, 87-88
    pension liability, 93-94
    Private Finance Initiative loans, 69
    Project Finacle IT investment, 26-29, 46, 51, 53, 66-68, 97-98
    Project Unity, 81
    Project Verde attempted purchase of Lloyds Bank branches, 45-58
    regulators' concerns, 30, 34-35, 37-38, 55-57, 75
    relationship with the Co-operative Group, 11, 25, 29, 40, 48, 71, 80, 82, 96
    results 2013, 68, 87
    risk profile, 30, 33, 35, 38, 49, 52
    sale of non-core assets, 64-65
    Smile, 28
    Treasury Select Committee hearings, 80-82, 101
    Unity Trust Bank, 69
    (*See also* Britannia Building Society, Co-operative Financial Services and Co-operative Group.
    For people see individual names.)

Co-operative Financial Services
   banking and insurance integration, 26-27, 28, 50, 51, 65-68, 98
   directors and board, 32
   Project Finacle IT investment, 26-29, 46, 51, 53, 66-68, 97-98
   relationship with the Co-operative Group, 24, 26-27
   use of building societies legislation, 24
   (*See also* Britannia Building Society, Co-operative
   Bank, Co-operative Group, Co-operative Insurance
   Society. *For people see individual names.*)
Co-operative Group, the (formerly Co-operative Wholesale Society)
   board and directors' involvement in decision making, 28, 98-99
   board changes, 79-84
   borrowing to fund purchases, 19
   business philosophy, 25
   convenience stores move, 18-19
   Co-operative Bank pension scheme separation, 94
   Co-operative Bank profits reliance, 53, 82
   financial position, 40, 52-58, 88
   general insurance business proposed sale, 20, 65
   governance, 19, 27-28, 79-84
   history, 11-14
   management, 11, 13-14
   Myners report on corporate governance, 19, 27-28, 98-99
   ownership of the Co-operative Bank, 11, 71, 76, 77, 88,
      91-93, 96-97
   Project Unity, 81
   Project Verde attempted purchase of Lloyds branches, 52, 58
   regulators' concerns about connections between businesses, 27
   relationship with Co-operative Bank, 11, 25, 29, 40, 48, 71, 80,
      82, 96
   relationship with Co-operative Financial Services, 26-27
   sale of pharmacy, farms and security businesses, 20, 57, 65
   scale of business strategy, 25, 46, 48
   Somerfield purchase, 18-20
   trading activity breadth, 19-20
   travel business, 20
   (*See also* Co-operative Bank and Co-operative
   Financial Services. *For people see individual names.*)

Co-operative Insurance Society, 26-27, 28, 50, 51, 65-68, 98
co-operative movement, 7, 11-14, 17
Co-operative Retail Services, 13
Co-operative Wholesale Society (*See* Co-operative Group, the)
Cyrus Capital, 95

Davies, David, 56
Dubai World, 73

Electoral Commission, 69
ethics
    Co-operative Bank policy, 7, 8-9, 52, 92, 94, 95, 96, 99
    co-operative movement, 7, 47

Financial Reporting Council, 41
financial sector economic cycles, 25
Financial Services Authority
    concerns at Britannia high-risk operations, 30, 34-35, 37-38
    concerns about attempted purchase of
    Lloyds Bank branches, 55-57
    criticism of activities and timing of warnings, 75
Financial Times, 55, 95
Fitch Ratings, 88-89
Fixed Income Investments, 72
Flowers, Paul, 9, 26, 47-54, 80-81, 101

Garnier, Mark, 82
Golden Tree Asset Management, 95
Goldman Sachs, 74
Guardian, 57

hedge funds and the Co-operative Bank, 72-77, 95, 96
HSBC, 83
Holt, Dennis, 94-95

insurance
    banking and insurance integration, 26-27, 28, 65-68, 98
    general insurance business proposed sale, 20, 65
    Payment Protection Insurance, 53, 68, 87, 92, 97

JC Flowers, 25, 77
J.P. Morgan Cazenove, 32

Kelly, Sir Christopher, Co-operative Bank review, 30-31, 66-67, 84
Kent Reliance Building Society, 24-25, 76
KPMG, 32

Labour Party, 69
Lloyds Bank 45-58, 82

McFall, Lord, 49
Marks, Peter
    CEO of the Co-operative Group, 14, 17-20, 34
    leadership, 17-18, 26, 57, 81, 100
    Lloyds Bank branches attempted purchase, 57-58, 80-81
    Project Unity, 80
    scale of business strategy, 25, 32, 45, 81
    Somerfield purchase, 18-20
    Treasury Select Committee, 80-82
Moelis, 75, 76
Moody's, 61-66, 99
Myners, Paul, 19, 27-28, 98-99

Nationwide, 83, 84
NBNK, 49
Northern Rock, 84
Norwich & Peterborough Building Society, 25-26, 98, 99

OneSavings Bank, 25

Payment Protection Insurance, 53, 68, 87, 92, 97
Pennell, Gerry, 67
pension liability of the Co-operative Bank, 93-94
Perry Capital, 89
Prescott, Alan, 26
Prudential Regulatory Authority, 32, 38-42, 55-56, 75, 76-77, 87-88
Pym, Richard, 68

Rees, Gareth, 42
Richardson, Neville, 28-29, 34-35, 38, 57, 80-81, 100
Rochdale Pioneers, 7
Royal Bank of Scotland, 83
Royal London, 66

Sainsbury's, 12, 18
Silver Point Capital, 73-75, 95
Smile, 28
Somerfield purchase, 18-20
Sunday Times, 69

Taber, Mark, 72, 74
Tesco, 12, 18
Tootell, Barry, 34, 39-42, 54, 57, 66, 80
Treasury Select Committee, 80-82, 101
Triodos Bank, 95

UBS bank, 76
Ulster Bank, 83
Unity Trust Bank, 69

Wardle, Len, 80, 81
Williams, Simon, 8

Yorkshire Building Society, 26, 83

www.ingramcontent.com/pod-product-compliance
Lightning Source LLC
Chambersburg PA
CBHW070304230526
45470CB00002B/708